Quinoa, Lentil & Radicchio
Salad (page 51)

Farro, Squash & Arugula Salad (page 50)

HEALTHY
INSTANT POT®

ALEXIS MERSEL

PHOTOGRAPHY BY

ERIN SCOTT

weldon**owen**

CONTENTS

Drunken Noodles with Beef (page 71)

Lemongrass & Garlic Pork Chops (page 68)

EATING WELL IS EASY

I wrote this book with a new baby (my first) at home. While I didn't underestimate the exhaustion associated with caring for a newborn (well, maybe a little), I completely miscalculated the multitasking. Needless to say, after our daughter was born, my Instant Pot® became my new best friend. In fact, the night of our daughter's first major meltdown, I was still able—amidst all the chaos—to cook Sesame Salmon with Soba Noodles (page 62) in minutes. I developed a new appreciation for the power of healthy, easy, set-and-forget-meals.

I've been a champion of my electric pressure cooker for a while, which led me to write and develop the first title in this series, *Everyday Instant Pot*. But the challenge of cooking healthy dishes while caring for a tiny human took my journey to the next level. The Instant Pot® makes eating well easy: lean proteins like chicken and fish are silky and tender; nutrient-packed beans don't need to be soaked; hearty grains and rice are fluffy but not mushy; and nourishing soups are surprisingly straightforward. Simply close the lid, forget about your meal, and focus on life's more important things.

Whether you're a first-time Instant Pot® user or an experienced pro in search of new healthy meals, this book is for you. Packed with more than sixty recipes, it has something for every lifestyle, including low-fat, low-sodium, gluten-free, dairy-free, paleo, vegetarian, and vegan dishes. You'll discover new ways to tackle classics, like swapping in zoodles for pasta in chicken soup, as well as some unexpected favorites—my husband loves the vegan lentil soup, despite his Midwestern meat-and-potato roots. And if you're in the mood for meat, the Korean Steak and Brown Rice Bowl (page 67) is a hearty, healthy choice.

As with any cooking tool, it's important to understand how the pot works before you start (see the primer on page 8). *Everyday Instant Pot* showed me how many people were so intimidated, they didn't even open the box. Please, open the box! The buttons and settings may seem confusing, but using your Instant-Pot® will become second nature. No matter what makes life chaotic, these easy recipes will build healthy eating into your busy lifestyle—and you'll never look back.

Bon appétit!

INSTANT POT® PRIMER

Welcome to a new world of fast, even, and flavorful cooking. The Instant Pot® cuts cooking to a fraction of the usual time, making traditionally long-simmering dishes at record speed. Meat is always tender and never dried out, because the pressure seals the liquid in the pot—and into the meat. Hearty grains and beans with typically long soaking and cooking times are ready for dinner without a lot of prep or planning. Soups come together in minutes, not hours, making a cozy weekend favorite possible any night of the week.

HOW DOES IT WORK?

The tightly sealed pot boils liquid quickly, then traps the steam and generates pressure. With pressure cooking, heat is very evenly, deeply, and quickly distributed. The machine is available in a selection of models and sizes, each with slightly different cooking features and programs. A general rule of thumb regarding size is if you're primarily cooking for four to six people, a model with a 6-quart (6-L) capacity should be sufficient, but if you're often feeding larger crowds of eight or more, an 8-quart (8-L) capacity might be more useful. The recipes in this book were developed and tested using the Duo Plus 6-Quart Instant Pot®. If you've just purchased an Instant Pot®, read the user manual first to get comfortable with your model's specific parts, buttons, settings, and indicator lights.

FUNCTIONS & SETTINGS

Each model has slightly different cooking features, with up to 18 different cooking programs to choose from, depending on the model. Since not all models have all settings, most of the recipes in this book use the manual pressure cook setting. Essentially, you can sauté, sear, steam, simmer, slow-cook, pressure-cook, and braise in this machine. The two most common functions used in these recipes are Pressure Cook and Sauté. You will discover that recipes often use both, with many starting with a sauté step followed by pressure cooking, or pressure cooking first and then finishing on the sauté function. It might seem like a lot of fuss, but once you get the hang of it, it won't feel that way at all. Just think about all the time and effort you are saving by not transferring food from pot to pot or stove to oven and back again! Most models also have settings specific to a type of food, such as Soup/Broth, Meat/Stew, Bean/Chili, Cake, Egg, Rice, Multigrain, Porridge, and Yogurt. These settings have built-in automatic programs set to the amount of time and pressure level needed for most dishes in that category, but you can adjust them as needed. Experiment with these for the recipes you cook often—they might help popular dishes in your household become truly set-and-forget meals. Some models also have a Sterilize

function, which can be used to sterilize bottles and jars easily and efficiently, but it is important to note that only the Max line of pots is safe for pressure canning. The Max also has a Sous Vide function, altitude adjustments, automated steam release, and a touch-screen interface.

Sauté: This function allows you to sear meat, simmer liquids, reduce sauces, and more, similar to how you would work with a sauté pan on the stove. It has three modes: Less is ideal for simmering, thickening, and reducing liquids; Normal is best for pan searing; More can be used for stir-frying or browning meat. The timer on this function is automatically set for thirty minutes, but in the rare case when you might need it on for longer than that, just press the Sauté button again after it has shut off and continue cooking. Never put the locking lid on while using it.

Pressure Cook: There are two levels for pressure cooking—High and Low. Most recipes utilize the High setting, but pay attention to when a recipe indicates using the Low setting (usually for more delicate foods like eggs or fish). Press the Pressure Level key or Adjust key (depending on your model) to adjust pressure levels, and the +/- keys to change the cooking time. (The Lux 6-in-1 V3 model does not have a low-pressure setting.)

Slow Cook: This is a non–pressure cooking program, where the Less, Normal, and High modes correspond to the low, medium, and high settings in some temperature-controlled slow cookers. It works similarly to a traditional slow-cooker appliance, cooking food very, very slowly with more liquid than required for pressure cooking. You can use this function for preparing your favorite slow-cooker recipes.

Steam: Always use the steam rack that came with the pot, or a metal or silicone steam basket, when using this program. The pot comes to pressure on full, continuous heat, and the food can scorch if it's not raised off the bottom of the pot.

Keep Warm/Cancel: These buttons, sometimes combined into one, turn off any cooking program, allowing you to switch to another program or to end cooking. The Keep Warm setting holds the food at a safe temperature for up to ten hours.

Delay Start: This feature allows you to delay the start of cooking, particularly handy if you want to soak beans before cooking them

UNDER PRESSURE

The pressure release (also called steam release) has two positions: Venting and Sealing. The pot can come up to pressure only when it is closed and the valve is set to Sealing. As a safety precaution, you will not be able to open the lid unless it is set to Venting. There are two main ways to release the pressure when the program ends:

Quick Release: Manually turn the valve to Venting as soon as the cooking program has ended. Take caution when moving the valve—it's best to use a wooden spoon or kitchen tongs instead of bare hands, and to not put your face over or near the valve since the steam will shoot out quickly.

Natural Release: The pot will lose pressure on its own as it cools. The time needed for a natural pressure release varies depending on the volume of food and liquid in the pot (the greater the amount, the longer it will take), and can be as quick as a few minutes or up to thirty. Once the program has finished, the pot defaults to the Keep Warm setting and will remain there for up to ten hours.

You can also perform a combination of the two, letting the pressure release naturally for a few minutes and then turning the valve to Venting to quick-release the rest of the steam. Each recipe in this book indicates the optimal method, whether it be quick release, natural, or a combination of the two. But it helps to understand why you are choosing one over another.

Two factors contribute to which method you would choose for steam release:

(1) Whether the dish is hearty and would benefit from sitting longer (such as a soup, stew, or braised meat dish), or if the dish involves delicate foods that require only a few minutes of cooking time (such as soft-boiled eggs, fish, or vegetables) and would not benefit from longer cooking or resting times.

(2) How much liquid is in the pot.

The first factor is often pretty straightforward: As many dishes in this book feature hearty ingredients, the majority will use a natural pressure release or a combination. The second factor is a safety issue. It's important to know that the steam releases quite intensely from the valve. With soups or other dishes containing a lot of liquid, there will be more steam releasing and more potential for hot water splattering over your kitchen or people nearby. Although it might be hard to wait a little longer to enjoy your meal after it has finished cooking, don't be hasty with releasing the steam manually. These recipes err on the side of caution when it comes to soups and other liquid-filled dishes.

LIQUID LEVELS

Unlike traditional slow cookers, which let liquids evaporate and reduce during cooking, a pressure cooker is completely sealed and therefore does not lose any steam when cooking. This is important because the amount of liquid needed for some recipes might seem low—but don't worry, they're correct for a 6-quart (6-L) pot. If you are using an 8-quart (8-L) pot, increase the liquid by 1 cup to avoid a Burn warning. The liquid level accounts for all wet ingredients, including stocks, water, wine, canned tomatoes with juice, marinades, and so on. The pot cannot come up to pressure unless it has enough liquid, so you'll want to make sure you have the minimum required for your model. Also, be sure to respect the fill line—to leave room for the steam buildup, the inner pot should never be more than two-thirds full.

PRESSURE COOKING PRACTICALITIES

- To come up to pressure, the pot needs enough steam buildup, which is created from the amount of liquid in the recipe. (Keep in mind that marinades and ingredients like canned tomatoes have liquid in them, too.)

- The valve might feel a bit wobbly when switching between Venting and Sealing.

- A little steam coming out of the valve is normal as the pot comes up to pressure.

- The program timer will not start until the machine has come up to pressure.

- For safety reasons, you cannot remove the lid from the pot when it is cooking under pressure. All of the pressure needs to be released first.

Ideal for health-minded menus, pressure cooking retains many nutrients that often get lost with other cooking methods. The recipes in this book feature meals for many lifestyles, including low-fat, low-sodium, gluten-free, dairy-free, paleo, vegetarian, and vegan dishes.

HEALTHY HOW-TOS

The recipes in this book offer a robust collection of good-for-you ideas for every meal of the day—including dessert! Use them to suit your lifestyle. For example, substitute gluten-free tamari for soy sauce, or leave out the cheese to create a vegan dish.

WHAT COOKS WELL IN THE INSTANT POT®

- Large cuts of meat emerge succulent and tender—especially tougher and less expensive cuts, which will not only save you money at the store but also time getting dinner on the table.

- Soups and stocks cook much more quickly, yet develop the same flavors as they would when simmered on the stove for hours.

- Rice, beans (which don't require soaking), and hearty grains are completely hands off—just throw everything into the pot and go.

- Steamed desserts are magically simple—no need to fuss with a hot-water bath in the oven or long cooking times. Steamed Stone Fruit Puddings (page 96) make the most of summer's fresh fruit bumper crop.

- Favorite breakfast dishes, such as steel-cut oats, are completely set-and-forget—perfect for busy mornings. In my version, coconut milk takes the place of regular milk (page 28).

- Risotto and polenta can be cooked without stirring at all, a huge help when you're multitasking in the kitchen. Try using nutrient-packed farro in place of Arborio rice in two seasonal risotto-style dishes (page 87).

Certain delicate foods need very little cooking time, or no pressure cooking at all. Tender vegetables can be cooked quickly on the Sauté mode, either at the beginning or end of cooking. Delicate fish and seafood only need a bit of simmering time in a soup or curry after all of the other ingredients are cooked and the dish flavors are developed. Eggs cook quickly (in some cases in as little as one minute) and often at low pressure. Rest assured that if any of your dishes come out undercooked for your preference, you can simply re-cover the pot, lock the lid, bring the machine back up to pressure, and cook for a few more minutes. Once the food in the pot is warm, it will take less time to come back up to pressure, so any additional cooking will be much quicker.

NUTRITIONAL KEY

Look for these icons to choose recipes suitable for specific dietary preferences.

- V VEGETARIAN
- GF GLUTEN-FREE
- P PALEO
- VG VEGAN
- DF DAIRY-FREE
- LS LOW SODIUM
- LF LOW FAT

Chicken Zoodle Soup (page 45)

SAUTÉING, SEARING & SIMMERING

The Instant Pot® Sauté program mimics how you would use a sauté pan or skillet on your stove—and it's one of the most useful features of the machine. Many meat dishes benefit from browning and searing before cooking, so you would begin a recipe in Sauté mode before pressure cooking.

Onions, shallots, garlic, celery, carrots, and other vegetables develop flavors when sautéed in some sort of fat (such as oil, butter, ghee, or animal fat), which will exponentially increase the flavors of your dish in many cases, especially when a spice blend is also tossed in. Try using avocado or coconut oil in place of canola oil. Another important use for this program is simmering sauces at the end of cooking. When the pot is in a pressure mode, no water will evaporate (unlike slow cooking or stovetop cooking), so reducing sauces for meats, curries, or creamy soups will not happen slowly over time. Instead, you can simmer them for a few minutes on Sauté mode after the pressure-cooking step, until the desired thickness is reached. Adding a slurry of equal parts cornstarch and water will help thicken sauces. (Always stir in cornstarch and flour at the end of cooking on Sauté mode—not at the beginning—before food has been pressure cooked, because it can settle and clump in the bottom of the inner pot, causing improper heat dispersion and scorching.)

TOOLS OF THE TRADE

A few key tools are essential to preparing a selection of recipes in this book. They include:

7-inch (18-cm) springform pan for cheesecake and other cakes

1½-quart (1.5-L) round oven-safe baking dish for frittatas, bread pudding, stuffing, and more "baked" dishes

Wire-mesh, silicone, or expandable metal steamer basket for potatoes, eggs, and vegetables

4-ounce (120-ml) ceramic ramekins for steamed desserts

Kitchen tongs for browning meat and transferring it from the pot to a plate; quick-releasing the steam valve safely; and holding a paper towel for removing fat from the pot after sautéing meat

Fat separator to degrease soups and sauces

Standard blender or immersion blender for soups, sauces, and marinades

Steam rack with handles to raise and lower pans and dishes, as well as for cooking eggs. (Note: This rack is included with many models; if yours does not have handles, you can create a sling by folding a long piece of aluminum foil into thirds so it can rest underneath the steam rack and extend up on either side like handles.)

TIPS & TRICKS

Many of the standard rules of cooking apply for pressure cooking, too, but the Instant Pot® also has a few guidelines of its own. It's helpful to read over a few key pointers to think about before you get started.

- Once you're familiar with the basics of your machine, the fun begins. Don't worry about feeling like a novice in the beginning—the more you use it, the more comfortable you'll become and increasingly able to customize recipes and cooking times to your preference.

- Cut ingredients into the same size so they cook evenly. This applies to everything from meat to vegetables. Size and cooking time are also related, as bigger pieces of meat will take longer to cook. Take note of the sizes listed for ingredients such as chicken, pork, beef, potatoes, and bread cubes, since cooking times are proportionate to the size of the ingredients.

- Cover cake pans, ramekins, and other dishes with aluminum foil when using a pressure setting so that condensation from the steam does not drip from the lid of the pot and water down your dish.

- Pat meat dry before cooking in fat, for better and more even browning.

- It's often easier and more time efficient to cook chicken pieces whole, then shred or cut them after cooking.

- Use kitchen tongs to hold paper towels to quickly and easily wipe out the fat from the inner pot during or after sautéing.

- Use kitchen tongs or a wooden spoon to carefully open the steam valve when releasing pressure so that your hands don't come in contact with hot steam.

- During steam release, ensure that the pot is at a safe distance from any surfaces that could be damaged by excess water, such as wooden cabinets. Always tilt the lid when removing it from the pot so steam doesn't hit your face.

- The inner pot can get quite hot while on Sauté mode, so sometimes smaller-sized ingredients will cook quickly and might start to stick or burn. If this happens, you can use stock, wine, or water to help deglaze the pot, stirring to loosen the browned bits from the pot bottom (many recipes include specific instructions for this). Use a wooden spoon and stir continually while sautéing to help prevent this from happening.

- Depending on the size of pot you have, the minimum amount of liquid required to create pressure will change. For a 3-quart (3-L) pot, the amount is 1½ cups (350 ml); for a 6-quart (6-L) pot it is 2 cups (475 ml); and for an 8-quart (8-L) pot, it is 3 cups (700 ml).

- Never fill the pot more than two-thirds full, to allow enough room for steam to build, or more than half full if cooking rice or beans, to give them room to expand.

- Adding cornstarch or flour before pressure cooking can result in settling and clumping at the bottom of the pot, which in turn can cause improper heat dispersion and scorching. Use cornstarch or flour to thicken sauces after pressure cooking to avoid this situation.

- If you find a marinade or sauce you like, try using it on a different meat or fish. The Korean marinade (page 67) would be equally delicious on chicken thighs or pork chops.

- Adding a few tablespoons of water when sautéing greens will help them to partially steam and prevent burning when using Sauté mode.

- You can add dried beans in soups because they will cook along with the other ingredients. They don't require soaking and taste much better than their canned counterparts.

- If you use homemade stock, which is likely to be less salty that store-bought, be sure to taste and add more salt after cooking, if needed.

- Buy and cook grains and beans in bulk—you'll save money, and you can use leftovers for quick weeknight meals or packable lunches.

- And finally, one of the most important rules of thumb for cooking is also essential here—taste your food and adjust the seasonings (salt, pepper, herbs, and spices) before you serve it. Season meat before browning or cooking, but also keep in mind that flavors develop throughout the cooking process, especially when simmering at the end of cooking. Use the salt and pepper quantities provided in the recipes as a guideline, and adjust for your preference.

Asian Chicken Salad with
Ginger Dressing (page 54)

Green Veggie Frittata (page 31)

BREAKFAST

Quinoa & Egg Breakfast Bowl

This warm, flavorful, and protein-packed grain bowl cooks in minutes, making it a powerful breakfast or midday meal. Prepare the toppings while the quinoa is in the pot, then arrange them over the bowls when it is ready.

SERVES 4

Put the quinoa, water, and salt in the Instant Pot®. Stir to combine.

Lock the lid in place and turn the valve to Sealing. Press the Pressure Cook button and set the cook time for 1 minute at high pressure.

Let the steam release naturally for 10 minutes, then turn the valve to Venting to quick-release any residual steam. Carefully remove the lid and fluff the quinoa with a fork.

To serve, divide the quinoa evenly among 4 bowls and place one egg on top of each bowl. Top the quinoa with the tomatoes, avocado, and seeds, sprinkle with salt and pepper, and serve right away.

1 cup (180 g) quinoa
(red, white, or mixed), rinsed

1¼ cups (300 ml) water

½ teaspoon salt

FOR SERVING

4 soft- or hard-boiled eggs
(page 109)

Cherry tomatoes, halved

Sliced avocado

Black sesame seeds or
"everything but the bagel"
seasoning

Flaked sea salt and freshly
ground black pepper

Add any of your favorite ingredients to these versatile bowls, such as nuts, seeds, beans, or steamed veggies.

Savory French Toast

Layered with sautéed asparagus and mushrooms then covered with a rich, herb-infused egg mixture, cubes of bread take on a dense, almost custard-like, texture.

SERVES 4-6

Grease a 1½-qt (1.5-L) ceramic baking dish with butter or cooking spray.

In a medium bowl, whisk together the eggs, milk, chives, basil, lemon zest, nutmeg, ¼ teaspoon salt, and ¼ teaspoon pepper. Set aside.

Select Sauté on the Instant Pot® and heat the oil. Add the asparagus, mushrooms, thyme, and ½ teaspoon salt and cook until the asparagus stems are bright green and the mushrooms begin to turn golden brown, about 5 minutes. Transfer to a plate. Press Cancel to reset the program.

Arrange one-third of the bread cubes in a single layer in the prepared baking dish. Layer half of the vegetable mixture on top. Place another third of the bread cubes in another layer on top, followed by the remaining vegetable mixture. Layer the remaining bread cubes on top and pour the egg mixture over all, pressing down gently so that the bread absorbs the liquid. Cover with aluminum foil and refrigerate for at least 1 hour or up to overnight.

Pour the water into the Instant Pot® and place the baking dish on the steam rack. Using the handles, lower the dish and steam rack into the pot. Lock the lid in place and turn the valve to Sealing. Press the Pressure Cook button and set the cook time for 30 minutes at high pressure.

Let the steam release naturally for 15 minutes, then turn the valve to Venting to quick-release any residual steam. Carefully remove the lid and, using the steam rack handles, lift out the dish. Transfer to a cooling rack, remove the foil, and let cool slightly. Cut into wedges and serve.

BONUS STEP *After removing it from the pot, sprinkle the savory French toast with Parmesan cheese and bake in a preheated 400°F (200°C) oven until golden brown, 8-10 minutes.*

Unsalted butter or cooking spray, for greasing

3 large eggs

2 cups (475 ml) whole milk

2 tablespoons chopped fresh chives

1 tablespoon chopped fresh basil

1 teaspoon freshly grated lemon zest

¼ teaspoon freshly grated nutmeg

Kosher salt and freshly ground black pepper

1 tablespoon canola or avocado oil

6 oz (180 g) asparagus, cut into 1-inch (2.5-cm) pieces

6 oz (180 g) cremini or white button mushrooms, sliced

1 teaspoon chopped fresh thyme leaves

8 oz (250 g) day-old baguette or country bread, cut into 1-inch (2.5-cm) cubes

2 cups (475 ml) water

Freshly grated Parmesan cheese (optional)

Yogurt Parfaits

The Instant Pot® is the secret weapon for making yogurt at home, creating creamy, full-fat yogurt that is significantly less tangy than store-bought varieties. Layered with your favorite seeds, nuts, and fruit, the almost sweet-tasting yogurt takes on a decidedly treat-like appeal.

SERVES 4

Pour the milk into the Instant Pot®. Lock the lid in place and turn the valve to Sealing. Press the Yogurt button until the screen says "Boil" and cook until the milk reaches 180°F (82°C), about 25 minutes. Have ready an ice-water bath in the sink. Carefully remove the lid and check the milk temperature with an instant-read thermometer. If it is not 180°F (82°C), press the Cancel button to reset the program, then select Sauté and heat until the milk temperature reaches 180°F (82°C). Transfer the inner pot to the ice-water bath, then stir the milk until it cools to 110°F (43°C), about 10 minutes. Transfer 1 cup (240 ml) of the milk to a small bowl, whisk in the yogurt until smooth, then return the milk-yogurt mixture to the pot. Whisk until blended.

Return the inner pot to the Instant Pot® housing. Lock the lid in place; the valve can be turned to Sealing or Venting. Press the Cancel button to reset the program, then press the Yogurt button and set the cook time for 10 hours. When the yogurt is ready (the screen will read "Yogt"), carefully remove the lid, use pot holders to lift out the inner pot, cover it with plastic wrap, and refrigerate until the yogurt sets, about 4 hours. Do not stir at this point.

When the yogurt is set, line a large fine-mesh sieve with 4 layers of cheesecloth, place the sieve over a bowl, spoon the yogurt into the sieve, and refrigerate for 2 hours to drain.

To serve, spoon some of the yogurt into the bottom of 4 medium-size glasses or jars. Top with a layer of seeds, nuts, and/or grains, followed by a layer of fruit. Repeat to fill all glasses.

8 cups (2 L) whole milk

2 tablespoons plain yogurt

FOR SERVING

Sunflower seeds, pepitas, toasted sliced almonds, chopped pecans, granola, puffed quinoa, and/or toasted coconut flakes

Fresh or dried stone fruit, fresh or dried berries

Coconut Milk Steel-Cut Oats

Rich, dense coconut milk is a tasty, dairy-free way to make your morning oats. Coconut milk is high in iron and zinc—good nutrients to support an active lifestyle—but feel free to substitute it with any of your favorite nut or dairy milks if you want to change things up.

SERVES 4

Combine the oats, coconut milk, water, and a pinch of salt in the Instant Pot® and stir to mix well.

Lock the lid in place and turn the valve to Sealing. Press the Pressure Cook button and set the cook time for 10 minutes at high pressure.

Let the steam release naturally for about 12 minutes, then turn the valve to Venting to quick-release any residual steam. Carefully remove the lid. Stir to combine the oats with any remaining liquid. To serve, spoon the oatmeal into individual bowls and top as desired.

1 cup (185 g) steel-cut oats

1 cup (240 ml) coconut milk

2 cups (475 ml) water

Kosher salt

TOPPINGS
Fresh or dried fruit, banana slices, honey, brown sugar, cinnamon, and/or cocoa powder

Egg Cups with Spinach & Sun-Dried Tomatoes

These individual egg cups are the perfect size for a breakfast on the go. You can add any of your favorite vegetables in place of the spinach and sun-dried tomatoes used here, as long as you cook any heartier veggie such as broccoli or kale in advance. For a lighter alternative, sub in egg whites for half of the eggs.

SERVES 4

Grease four 6-oz (180-ml) mason jars or ramekins with nonstick cooking spray.

In a medium bowl, whisk the eggs. Stir in the spinach, tomatoes, goat cheese, chives, ½ teaspoon salt, and ¼ teaspoon pepper. Pour the egg mixture into the prepared jars, dividing it evenly. Cover each with aluminum foil.

Pour the water into the Instant Pot® and place the mason jars on the steam rack. Using the handles, lower the jars and steam rack into the pot. Lock the lid in place and turn the valve to Sealing. Press the Pressure Cook button and set the cook time for 5 minutes at low pressure.

When the eggs have finished cooking, turn the valve to Venting to quick-release the steam. Carefully remove the lid and, using the steam rack handles, lift out the jars.

Serve warm, or seal with the mason jar lids (or plastic wrap) and store in the refrigerator for up to 3 days.

Nonstick cooking spray

8 eggs

1 cup (60 g) chopped spinach

¼ cup (25 g) sun-dried tomatoes, chopped

¼ cup (40 g) crumbled goat cheese

1 tablespoon chopped chives

Kosher salt and freshly ground black pepper

2 cups (500 ml) water

Green Veggie Frittata

Kale, zucchini, and a trio of green herbs contribute fresh flavor to this hearty breakfast. Cut the frittata into wedges to serve as part of a weekend brunch, reserving any leftovers for easy grab-and-go breakfasts through the week.

SERVES 6

Grease a 1½-qt (1.5-L) round ceramic baking dish with butter or cooking spray. In a large bowl, whisk together the eggs, milk, ½ teaspoon salt, and ¼ teaspoon pepper. Set aside.

Select Sauté on the Instant Pot® and heat the oil. Add the shallot and cook until just softened, 1 minute. Add the kale, ¼ teaspoon salt, and 2 tablespoons of the water and cook, stirring occasionally with a wooden spoon and scraping up any browned bits, until the kale has started to soften and brown in some spots, about 3 minutes. Add the zucchini and 1 tablespoon water and cook for 3 minutes more.

Press the Cancel button to reset the program. Transfer the vegetable mixture to the egg mixture and stir to combine. Fold in the herbs and cheese. Pour into the prepared baking dish. Cover with aluminum foil.

Pour the 2 cups (475 ml) water into the Instant Pot® and place the baking dish on the steam rack. Using the handles, lower the baking dish and steam rack into the pot. Lock the lid in place and turn the valve to Sealing. Press the Pressure Cook button and set the cook time for 17 minutes at high pressure.

Let the steam release naturally for 10 minutes, then turn the valve to Venting to quick-release any residual steam. Carefully remove the lid and, using the steam rack handles, lift out the baking dish. Let the frittata cool slightly before cutting it into wedges and serving. Alternatively, remove the entire frittata from the baking dish by sliding a butter knife along the edges to loosen it. Place a plate on top of the baking dish, invert it, and shake gently to loosen the frittata onto the plate. Using a spatula, flip the frittata right-side up onto the plate. Cut into wedges and serve.

Unsalted butter or cooking spray, for greasing

8 large eggs

¾ cup (180 ml) whole milk

Kosher salt and freshly ground black pepper

1 tablespoon canola or avocado oil

1 large shallot, sliced

4 oz (115 g) kale, chopped

2 cups (475 ml) plus 3 tablespoons water

1 zucchini, thinly sliced

1 tablespoon chopped fresh flat-leaf parsley

1 tablespoon chopped fresh dill

1 tablespoon minced fresh chives

1 cup (120 g) shredded mozzarella cheese

Asian Chicken Salad with
Ginger Dressing (page 54)

SOUPS & SALADS

Summer Garden Soup

This chunky vegetable soup features some of summer's favorite ingredients—tomatoes, zucchini, and corn. Best of all, incorporating easy-to-find vegetables means it can be enjoyed all year long. Top each bowl with a sprinkling of chopped fresh basil just before serving.

SERVES 6

Select Sauté on the Instant Pot® and heat the oil. Add the onion and cook, stirring occasionally, until softened, about 5 minutes. Add the garlic and cook until fragrant, 1 minute. Add the tomatoes and their juices, breaking up the tomatoes with a wooden spoon, the oregano, 2 teaspoons salt, and ½ teaspoon pepper and cook until blended, 1 minute. Press the Cancel button to reset the program.

Add the stock and zucchini to the pot. Lock the lid in place and turn the valve to Sealing. Press the Pressure Cook button and set the cook time for 20 minutes at high pressure.

Let the steam release naturally, or for at least 15 minutes, before turning the valve to Venting to quick-release any residual steam. Carefully remove the lid.

While the soup is still hot, add the corn and cook until it is heated through, about 2 minutes. Taste and adjust the seasoning as needed.

Ladle the soup into bowls, sprinkle with basil, and serve right away.

2 tablespoons olive oil

1 yellow onion, chopped

5 cloves garlic, minced

1 can (28 oz/800 g) whole peeled tomatoes

½ teaspoon oregano

Kosher salt and freshly ground black pepper

3 cups (700 ml) vegetable stock (page 121 or store-bought)

2 zucchini, halved lengthwise and sliced 1 inch (2.5 cm) thick

1 cup (180 g) fresh or frozen corn kernels (about 2 ears)

FOR SERVING
Fresh chopped basil

*Charred corn tortillas make
a delicious accompaniment.
Brown them in a dry frying pan
on the stovetop before serving.*

Pozole Rojo with Pork

This classic Mexican comfort food comes together quickly in the Instant Pot®. Prepare the toppings while it cooks, then set them out in pretty bowls with the finished soup. Mexican oregano has a citrusy appeal that works well with south-of-the-border flavors, though any type of oregano will work in this dish.

SERVES 6

Season the pork generously with salt and pepper. Select Sauté on the Instant Pot® and heat 1 tablespoon of the oil. Working in batches, add the pork and brown evenly on both sides, about 3 minutes per side. Transfer to a plate as browned.

Add the remaining tablespoon of oil and the onion and cook, stirring occasionally with a wooden spoon and scraping up any browned bits, until softened, about 3 minutes. Add the garlic and cook until fragrant, about 1 minute. Add the tomato paste, chili powder, oregano, thyme, and 2 tablespoons of the stock and cook for 1 minute. Press the Cancel button to reset the program.

Add the remaining stock, the water, and the hominy and stir. Return the pork and its juices to the pot. Lock the lid in place and turn the valve to Sealing. Press the Pressure Cook button and set the cook time for 30 minutes at high pressure.

Let the steam release naturally for 20 minutes, then turn the valve to Venting to quick-release any residual steam. Carefully remove the lid and transfer the pork to a plate. Let the meat cool slightly and then shred it into bite-size pieces. Return the shredded pork to the pot. Add 1 teaspoon salt. Taste and add more salt and pepper, if desired.

Ladle into bowls and add desired toppings. Serve with charred corn tortillas and lime wedges alongside.

2 lb (1 kg) boneless thick-cut pork chops (about 4), excess fat trimmed

Kosher salt and freshly ground black pepper

2 tablespoons canola or avocado oil

1 large onion, chopped

8 cloves garlic, minced

2 tablespoons tomato paste

2 tablespoons chili powder

1½ teaspoons dried oregano, preferably Mexican

½ teaspoon dried thyme

4 cups (1 L) chicken stock (page 120 or store-bought)

1 cup (240 ml) water

1 can (25 oz/700 g) hominy, rinsed and drained

FOR SERVING
Shredded green cabbage, thinly sliced radishes, diced onions (red, yellow, or white), sour cream, cilantro leaves, charred corn tortillas, lime wedges

Carrot Soup with Toasted Pepitas & Cilantro

Fresh-tasting carrot soup is an easy addition to any health-minded menu. Make a big batch and freeze in 1-cup containers that are easy to thaw and reheat for a quick and nutritious snack or lunch on demand.

SERVES 6

Select Sauté on the Instant Pot® and heat the oil. Add the onion and cook, stirring occasionally, until softened, about 5 minutes. Add the garlic and cook until fragrant, 1 minute. Add the carrots, 2 teaspoons salt, and ½ teaspoon pepper and cook until blended, 2 minutes. Press the Cancel button to reset the program.

Add the stock, orange juice, and ginger to the pot. Lock the lid in place and turn the valve to Sealing. Press the Pressure Cook button and set the cook time for 20 minutes at high pressure.

Let the steam release naturally, or for at least 15 minutes, before turning the valve to Venting to quick-release any residual steam. Carefully remove the lid.

Using an immersion blender (or transferring the soup in batches to a blender), purée the soup until smooth. Taste and adjust the seasoning as needed.

Ladle the soup into bowls, sprinkle with toasted pepitas and cilantro, and serve right away.

1 tablespoon olive oil

1 yellow onion, chopped

2 cloves garlic, minced

1½ lb (680 g) carrots, peeled and cut into slices ¼ inch (6 mm) thick

Kosher salt and freshly ground black pepper

4 cups (1 L) vegetable stock (page 121 or store-bought)

¼ cup (60 ml) orange juice

2 teaspoons peeled and grated fresh ginger

FOR SERVING
Toasted pepitas (pumpkin seeds)

Freshly chopped cilantro

Smoky Black Bean Soup with Tangy Crema

This robust yet simple-to-prepare soup comes together quickly when cooked under pressure. The beans simmer to perfection without presoaking, taking on the flavor of the herbs, spices, and smoky-flavored adobo sauce in the process.

SERVES 6

Select Sauté on the Instant Pot® and heat the oil. Add the yellow onion and bell pepper and cook until softened, about 5 minutes. Add the jalapeño, garlic, adobo sauce, cumin, paprika, oregano, and 1 teaspoon salt and cook until fragrant, about 2 minutes. Add the beans and stock and stir to combine.

Lock the lid in place and turn the valve to Sealing. Press the Pressure Cook button and set the cook time for 45 minutes at high pressure.

While the soup cooks, make the crema. In a small bowl, combine the sour cream, cilantro, red onion, lime zest, 1 tablespoon of the lime juice, ½ teaspoon salt, and a few grindings of fresh pepper and stir to combine. Taste and adjust the seasoning as needed.

When the soup has finished cooking, let the steam release naturally for about 15 minutes, then turn the valve to Venting to quick-release any residual steam and carefully remove the lid. Stir the remaining 1 tablespoon lime juice and a few grindings of fresh pepper into the soup. Taste and adjust the seasoning as needed.

Ladle the soup into bowls and top each with a large spoonful of the crema, garnish with more cilantro, and serve with tortilla chips alongside.

1 tablespoon canola or avocado oil

1 yellow onion, diced

1 red bell pepper, seeded and diced

1 jalapeño chile, seeded and minced

3 cloves garlic, minced

1 tablespoon adobo sauce from canned chipotle chiles

1 tablespoon ground cumin

1½ teaspoons smoked paprika

1 teaspoon dried oregano

Kosher salt and freshly ground black pepper

1 lb (450 g) dried black beans, picked over and rinsed

4 cups (1 L) vegetable stock (page 121 or store-bought)

FOR THE CREMA
1 cup (225 g) sour cream

¼ cup (7 g) chopped fresh cilantro, plus more for garnish

¼ cup (45 g) minced red onion

1 teaspoon grated lime zest

2 tablespoons fresh lime juice

Tortilla chips, for serving

Chicken & White Bean Soup

Pressure cooking beans takes a fraction of the time it would on the stovetop, without having to soak them first. Mixed here with spices, corn, and chicken, this hearty soup is a light and healthy alternative to more traditional recipes. You can purée half of the soup before serving for thick, chili-like texture.

SERVES 6

Select Sauté on the Instant Pot® and heat the oil. Add the onion and cook, stirring occasionally, until softened, about 5 minutes. Add the garlic and cook until fragrant, 1 minute. Add the chili powder, cumin, 1 teaspoon salt, and ¼ teaspoon pepper and stir to combine. Press the Cancel button to reset the program.

Add the stock, canned chiles and their juices, beans, chicken, and bay leaves to the pot. Lock the lid in place and turn the valve to Sealing. Press the Pressure Cook button and set the cook time for 30 minutes at high pressure.

Let the steam release naturally, or for at least 15 minutes, before turning the valve to Venting to quick-release any residual steam. Carefully remove the lid. Remove and discard the bay leaves.

While the soup is still hot, add the corn and cook until it is heated through, about 2 minutes. Taste and adjust the seasoning as needed.

Ladle the soup into bowls and top with avocado, jalapeño, and cilantro. Serve right away with tortilla chips alongside.

1 tablespoon olive oil

1 yellow onion, chopped

4 cloves garlic, minced

1 tablespoon chili powder

2 teaspoons ground cumin

Kosher salt and freshly ground black pepper

5 cups (1.25 L) chicken stock (page 120 or store-bought)

1 can (4 oz/115 g) diced green chiles

1 cup (200 g) dried great white or northern beans, picked over and rinsed

1½ lb (680 g) boneless, skinless chicken breasts

2 bay leaves

1 cup (180 g) fresh or frozen corn kernels (about 2 ears)

FOR SERVING
Avocado (sliced or diced), sliced jalapeño chile, cilantro, tortilla chips

Sprinkle each bowl with ground Aleppo pepper for an extra hit of flavor and color before serving.

Double Kale & Bean Soup

Add two varieties of kale—Tuscan and curly—for a more varied flavor and texture in this hearty cannellini bean soup. Grate the Parmesan cheese for serving in advance so you can slip the cheese rind into the pot with the beans to enhance the soup's flavor and texture.

SERVES 6

Select Sauté on the Instant Pot® and heat the oil. Add the onion, carrots, and celery and cook, stirring occasionally, until softened, about 5 minutes. Add the garlic and cook until fragrant, 1 minute. Add the tomatoes and their juices, breaking up the tomatoes with a wooden spoon, the oregano, red pepper flakes, 2 teaspoons salt, and ½ teaspoon pepper and cook until blended, 1 minute. Press the Cancel button to reset the program.

Add the stock, beans, bay leaf, Parmesan rind, and water to the pot. Lock the lid in place and turn the valve to Sealing. Press the Pressure Cook button and set the cook time for 40 minutes at high pressure.

Let the steam release naturally, or for at least 15 minutes, before turning the valve to Venting to quick-release any residual steam. Carefully remove the lid. Remove and discard the bay leaf and Parmesan rind.

Press the Sauté button, add the kale, and cook until it is wilted and heated through, about 5 minutes. Taste and adjust the seasoning as needed.

Ladle the soup into bowls, sprinkle with parsley and cheese, and serve right away.

2 tablespoons olive oil

1 yellow onion, chopped

2 carrots, peeled and chopped

2 ribs celery, sliced

4 cloves garlic, minced

1 can (14.5 oz/410 g) diced tomatoes

1 teaspoon dried oregano

¼ teaspoon red pepper flakes

Kosher salt and freshly ground black pepper

4 cups (1 L) vegetable stock (page 121 or store-bought)

1 cup (200 g) dried cannellini beans, picked over and rinsed

1 bay leaf

1 Parmesan cheese rind

1 cup (240 ml) water

12 oz (about 4 cups) Tuscan and/or curly kale, thick stems and ribs removed, chopped

FOR SERVING
Chopped fresh flat-leaf parsley

Freshly grated Parmesan cheese

Classic Lentil Soup

The classic soup base trio—onion, carrots, and celery—remains refreshingly firm in this staple recipe. A shot of red wine vinegar added just before serving balances the rich flavors, but the soup is also delicious without it. Stir in chunks of cooked diced ham or turkey bacon for a hearty, subtly smoky profile, if you like.

SERVES 4–6

Select Sauté on the Instant Pot® and heat the oil. Add the onion, carrots, celery, 2 teaspoons salt, and ½ teaspoon pepper and cook, stirring occasionally, until softened, about 5 minutes. Add the garlic and thyme and cook until fragrant, 1 minute. Add the tomatoes with their juices, breaking up the tomatoes with a wooden spoon, followed by the water, lentils, and bay leaf. Cook until combined, 2 minutes. Press the Cancel button to reset the program.

Lock the lid in place and turn the valve to Sealing. Press the Pressure Cook button and set the cook time for 15 minutes at high pressure.

Let the steam release naturally, or for at least 15 minutes, before turning the valve to Venting to quick-release any residual steam. Carefully remove the lid. Stir in the vinegar, if desired. Remove and discard the bay leaf. Taste and adjust the seasoning as needed.

Ladle into bowls and serve right away.

1 tablespoon olive oil

1 yellow onion, chopped

3 carrots, peeled and chopped

3 ribs celery, sliced

Kosher salt and freshly ground black pepper

3 cloves garlic, minced

½ teaspoon dried thyme

1 can (28 oz/800 g) whole peeled tomatoes

4 cups (1 L) water

1 cup (200 g) green or black lentils, picked over and rinsed

1 bay leaf

1 tablespoon red wine vinegar (optional)

Sample one bowl with these crisp-tender cooked zoodles and you may never go back to regular noodles again.

Chicken Zoodle Soup

This soup cooks in a little more than 10 minutes, but tastes as if it has simmered for hours. Zucchini "zoodles" replace traditional pasta noodles for a healthful spin on the classic recipe. Look for packaged precut zoodles in the produce section, make your own with a spiralizer, or cut strips with a vegetable peeler.

SERVES 6

Put the onion, carrots, celery, broth, bay leaf, vinegar, parsley sprigs, thyme, and 1 teaspoon salt in the Instant Pot®. Stir to combine. Nestle the chicken inside.

Lock the lid in place and turn the valve to Sealing. Press the Pressure Cook button and set the cook time for 8 minutes at high pressure.

Turn the valve to Venting to quick-release the steam. Carefully remove the lid. Transfer the chicken breasts to a plate. Let the meat cool slightly and then shred it with two forks. While the soup is still hot, add the zucchini noodles to the pot and heat for 3 minutes until they are warmed through. Remove and discard the bay leaf and parsley sprigs. Return the shredded chicken and its juices to the pot and stir to combine.

Taste and adjust the seasoning as needed. Ladle into bowls, sprinkle with parsley leaves and pepper, and serve right away.

1 medium onion, chopped

2 carrots, peeled, sliced ½ inch (12 mm) thick

3 ribs celery, sliced ½ inch (12 mm) thick

6 cups (1.5 L) chicken stock (page 120 or store-bought)

1 bay leaf

1 tablespoon apple cider vinegar

1 bunch fresh flat-leaf parsley, leaves and sprigs separated, sprigs tied together with kitchen twine, leaves reserved for garnish

1½ teaspoons chopped fresh thyme leaves (or ¾ teaspoon dried thyme)

Kosher salt and freshly ground black pepper

1 lb (500 g) boneless, skinless chicken breasts

2 zucchini, spiralized or cut into ribbons using a vegetable peeler, or 1 package (10 oz/280 g) zucchini noodles ("zoodles")

Chicken Meatball & Barley Soup

Italian-spiced chicken meatballs combine with onion, barley, and Swiss chard in this addictive winter soup. Swap in any hearty green, such as kale or mustard greens, in place of the chard, and skip the Parmesan when making the meatballs if you would like to make the soup dairy-free.

SERVES 6

To make the meatballs, in a medium bowl, combine the chicken, garlic, bread crumbs, cheese, egg, tomato paste, oregano, 1 teaspoon salt, and ¼ teaspoon pepper. Using your hands or a wooden spoon, stir gently to combine (be careful not to overmix, or the meat will become tough). Take a heaping teaspoon of meat and, using slightly wet hands, roll it between your palms to form a ball. Place each ball on a plate and set aside. (You should have about 30 meatballs.)

Select Sauté on the Instant Pot® and heat the oil. Add the onion and cook, stirring occasionally, until softened, about 5 minutes. Add the garlic and cook until fragrant, 1 minute. Add the tomato paste, 1 teaspoon salt, and ¼ teaspoon pepper and cook until blended, 1 minute. Press the Cancel button to reset the program.

Add the barley, stock, and meatballs to the pot. Lock the lid in place and turn the valve to Sealing. Press the Pressure Cook button and set the cook time for 20 minutes at high pressure.

Let the steam release naturally for 10 minutes before turning the valve to Venting to quick-release any residual steam. Carefully remove the lid.

While the soup is still hot, add the chard and cook until it is wilted, about 3 minutes. Taste and adjust the seasoning as needed.

Ladle the soup into bowls and serve right away.

FOR THE MEATBALLS

1 lb (450 g) ground chicken or turkey

2 cloves garlic, minced or grated

¼ cup (25 g) panko bread crumbs

2 tablespoons grated Parmesan cheese

1 egg, lightly beaten

1 tablespoon tomato paste

1 teaspoon dried oregano

Kosher salt and freshly ground black pepper

2 tablespoons olive oil

1 yellow onion, chopped

2 cloves garlic, minced

2 tablespoons tomato paste

1 cup (180 g) barley, rinsed well and drained

6 cups (1.5 L) chicken stock (page 120 or store-bought)

1 large bunch Swiss chard, thick stems and ribs removed, cut into 1-inch (2.5-cm) pieces

Red Curry Shrimp Soup

The Instant Pot® is a master at quickly concentrating flavors, like those extracted from the fragrant Thai ingredients in this noodle soup. For the perfect finish to the steaming bowls, fry thinly sliced shallots in hot oil until golden and crisp, then scatter the crispy shallots on top.

SERVES 4

Combine the stock, coconut milk, curry paste, ginger, garlic, shallots, lime leaves, chile (if desired), and 1 teaspoon salt in the Instant Pot®. Stir to combine.

Lock the lid in place and turn the valve to Sealing. Press the Pressure Cook button and set the cook time for 20 minutes at high pressure.

Meanwhile, cook the noodles according to the package directions and set aside.

Let the steam release naturally for 10 minutes, then turn the valve to Venting to quick-release any residual steam. Carefully remove the lid. While the soup is still hot, add the shrimp to the pot and heat for 2–3 minutes until they turn pink and opaque. (If using frozen shrimp, heat for about 5 minutes.) Remove and discard the lime leaves. Add the lime juice to the pot and stir to combine.

Taste and adjust the seasoning as needed. To serve, divide the noodles evenly among 4 bowls, ladle the soup on top, and sprinkle with a few basil leaves.

4 cups (1 L) chicken or vegetable stock (page 120 or store-bought)

1 can (13.5 oz/400 ml) full-fat coconut milk

2 tablespoons red curry paste

1 teaspoon peeled and grated fresh ginger

1 clove garlic, minced

3 shallots, sliced

3 Thai lime leaves

1 red Thai chile, seeded and minced (optional)

Kosher salt

1 package (8 oz/250 g) dried rice noodles

1 lb (450 g) shrimp, fresh or frozen, peeled and deveined

2 tablespoons fresh lime juice

Thai basil leaves, for serving

Spicy Seafood Soup

Tomatoes, herbs, a hint of orange, and a handful of alliums—onion, leek, fennel, and garlic—form the flavorful base for this nourishing soup. Shrimp and fish are added to the hot broth at the end so they cook quickly and stay tender.

SERVES 6

Select Sauté on the Instant Pot® and heat the oil. Add the onion, leek, and fennel and cook, stirring occasionally, until softened, about 5 minutes. Add the garlic and tomatoes with their juices, breaking up the tomatoes with a wooden spoon. Cook until combined, 3 minutes. Add the clam juice, water, bay leaf, saffron (if using), red pepper flakes, thyme, orange zest, 1 teaspoon salt, and ½ teaspoon pepper and bring to a simmer, stirring occasionally with a wooden spoon. Press the Cancel button to reset the program.

Lock the lid in place and turn the valve to Sealing. Press the Pressure Cook button and set the cook time for 20 minutes at high pressure.

Let the steam release naturally, or for at least 15 minutes, before turning the valve to Venting to quick-release any residual steam. Carefully remove the lid. Remove and discard the bay leaf.

Press the Sauté button and add the fish. Cook until opaque, about 3 minutes. Add the shrimp and cook until they turn pink and opaque, 2–3 minutes more. (If using frozen shrimp, cook for about 5 minutes.) Taste and adjust the seasoning as needed.

Ladle into bowls and top with reserved fennel fronds and parsley. Sprinkle with pepper and serve right away with grilled bread alongside.

2 tablespoons olive oil

1 yellow onion, chopped

1 leek, thinly sliced

½ fennel bulb, thinly sliced (reserve fronds for serving)

4 cloves garlic, minced

1 can (28 oz/800 g) whole peeled tomatoes

2 cups (475 ml) clam juice

2 cups (475 ml) water

1 bay leaf

2 pinches saffron threads (optional)

¼ teaspoon red pepper flakes

1 teaspoon dried thyme

1 teaspoon freshly grated orange zest

Kosher salt and freshly ground black pepper

1 lb (500 g) white fish (see note at right), skinned and cut into 2-inch (5-cm) pieces

1 lb (500 g) shrimp, fresh or frozen, peeled and deveined

FOR SERVING

Chopped fennel fronds, chopped fresh flat-leaf parsley, grilled crusty bread

Use any of your favorite white fish varieties in this dish, such as tilapia, halibut, cod, or a combination.

Farro, Squash & Arugula Salad

These colorful grain bowls are packed full of fiber, nutrients, and a fresh mix of textures and flavors. For a quick and healthy lunch on the go, pack the salad into large jars or other airtight containers, storing the dressing in a separate container to toss in just before eating.

SERVES 4

Prepare the farro as directed.

Pour the water into the Instant Pot®. Place the squash slices in a steamer basket or ovenproof bowl and set it on the steam rack. Using the handles, lower the steamer basket and steam rack into the pot. Lock the lid in place and turn the valve to Sealing. Press the Pressure Cook button and set the cook time for 4 minutes at high pressure.

Meanwhile, make the dressing. In a small lidded jar, combine the orange juice, lemon juice, vinegar, olive oil, sugar, and a pinch of salt. Close the lid and shake well until blended. Add more salt, if needed, and pepper to taste. Set aside.

When the squash has finished cooking, turn the valve to Venting to quick-release the steam. When the steam stops, carefully remove the lid and, using the steam rack handles, lift out the steamer basket.

To serve, divide the farro evenly among 4 plates or large bowls. Top the farro with squash, arugula, radish slices, pomegranate seeds, and pepitas. Use a vegetable peeler to shave large pieces of cheese on top. Sprinkle with salt and a few grindings of black pepper. Drizzle some of the dressing on top and serve with the remaining dressing alongside.

2 cups (360 g) cooked farro (page 115)

1 cup (240 ml) water

1 large delicata squash (about 1 lb/450 g), halved and cut into pieces 1 inch (2.5 cm) wide

FOR THE DRESSING
¼ cup (60 ml) fresh orange juice

1 tablespoon fresh lemon juice

1 tablespoon champagne vinegar

½ cup (120 ml) olive oil

¼ teaspoon sugar

Kosher salt and freshly ground black pepper

2 cups (60 g) arugula

2 watermelon or other radishes, thinly sliced

¼ cup (40 g) pomegranate seeds

¼ cup (40 g) toasted pepitas (pumpkin seeds)

Wedge of Parmesan or pecorino romano cheese, for shaving

Quinoa, Lentil & Radicchio Salad

Enjoy this protein-packed salad at lunch for enough fuel to last through the day. Crumbled goat cheese contributes a mellow creaminess to the hearty bean-and-grain mix. Use the softest variety you can find so it blends in easily. If making the salad ahead, don't add the apple or dressing until just before serving.

SERVES 4

Prepare the quinoa as directed.

Put the lentils, water, and ½ teaspoon salt in the Instant Pot®. Stir to combine. Lock the lid in place and turn the valve to Sealing. Press the Pressure Cook button and set the cook time for 10 minutes at high pressure.

Meanwhile, make the dressing. Combine the vinegar, honey, olive oil, and a pinch of salt in a small lidded jar. Close the lid and shake well until blended. Add more salt, if needed, and pepper to taste. Set aside.

When the lentils have finished cooking, let the steam release naturally for 10 minutes, then turn the valve to Venting to quick-release any residual steam. Carefully remove the lid.

To serve, divide the quinoa evenly among 4 plates or large bowls. Top the quinoa with a scoop of lentils (reserve any remaining lentils for another meal), radicchio, apple slices, goat cheese, and basil. Sprinkle with salt and a few grindings of black pepper. Drizzle some of the dressing on top and serve with the remaining dressing alongside.

2 cups (370 g) cooked red, white, or mixed quinoa (page 114)

1 cup (200 g) black lentils, picked over and rinsed

2 cups (475 ml) water

Kosher salt and freshly ground black pepper

FOR THE DRESSING
¼ cup (60 ml) apple cider vinegar

2 tablespoons honey

⅓ cup (80 ml) olive oil

1 head radicchio, cored and sliced into strips

1 Pink Lady or other red-skinned apple, cored and thinly sliced

½ cup (80 g) crumbled goat cheese

Chopped fresh basil

Farro, Squash & Arugula
Salad (page 50)

Robust salads packed
with hearty beans and
grains are balanced by
flavorful additions such
as seeds, nuts, crisp
apples, sliced radishes,
and creamy goat cheese.

Quinoa, Lentil & Radicchio
Salad (page 51)

Asian Chicken Salad with Ginger Dressing

Fragrant ginger-marinated chicken pairs beautifully with wild rice, blood orange, and red cabbage in this colorful salad. Garnish with fresh cilantro leaves.

SERVES 4

To make the marinade, in a small bowl or measuring cup, whisk together the tamari, sesame oil, vinegar, and ginger. Place the chicken breasts in a shallow pan or baking dish and pour the marinade over the top. Cover with plastic wrap and marinate in the refrigerator for at least 30 minutes and up to 2 hours, turning occasionally to coat.

Select Sauté on the Instant Pot® and heat the oil. Working in batches, add the chicken breasts, reserving the marinade, and brown evenly on both sides, 2–3 minutes per side. Add the stock and use a wooden spoon to scrape up any browned bits. Add the reserved marinade and stir to combine. Press the Cancel button to reset the program.

Lock the lid in place and turn the valve to Sealing. Press the Pressure Cook button and set the cook time for 6 minutes at high pressure.

Meanwhile, to make the dressing, put the vinegar, tamari, brown sugar, ginger, pepper, and canola oil in a blender or food processor and blend until smooth. Set aside.

When the chicken has finished cooking, let the steam release naturally for 5 minutes, before turning the valve to Venting to quick-release any residual steam.

Carefully remove the lid and use tongs to transfer the chicken to a plate. Let the meat cool slightly and then shred it with two forks.

Divide the rice, lettuce, cabbage, chicken, oranges, and peanuts evenly among 4 plates. Serve with dressing alongside.

FOR THE MARINADE

¼ cup (60 ml) tamari

2 teaspoons toasted sesame oil

2 teaspoons rice vinegar

2 tablespoons grated fresh ginger

1½ lb (680 g) boneless, skinless chicken breasts

1 tablespoon canola oil

½ cup (120 ml) chicken stock (page 120 or store-bought)

FOR THE DRESSING

2 tablespoons rice vinegar

1 tablespoon tamari

1 tablespoon brown sugar

2 tablespoons grated fresh ginger

¼ teaspoon freshly ground black pepper

¼ cup (60 ml) canola oil

FOR SERVING

Wild Rice (page 113)

4 cups (200 g) romaine lettuce, chopped

2 cups (200 g) shredded red cabbage

2 blood or navel oranges

½ cup (75 g) roasted peanuts

Blood oranges make a flavorful—
and beautiful—addition to this
salad, but you can use any orange
variety that you find.

Lemongrass & Garlic Pork Chops (page 68)

MAINS

Salmon Tacos with Crispy Slaw

Salmon develops an irresistible, silky texture when cooked quickly on the steam setting. Topped with a citrusy slaw of nutrient-rich brussels sprouts and cabbage, these will likely become your new favorite tacos.

SERVES 4

In a small bowl, mix the chile powder, cumin, coriander, ½ teaspoon salt, and ¼ teaspoon pepper. Place the salmon in a shallow pan or on a plate and rub spice mixture over the non-skin side of the salmon.

Pour the water into the Instant Pot® and place the salmon, skin-side down, on the steam rack. Using the handles, lower the steam rack into the pot. Lock the lid in place and turn the valve to Sealing. Press the Steam button and set the cook time for 3 minutes.

Meanwhile, make the slaw and crema. To make the slaw, combine the brussels sprouts, cabbage, onion, cilantro, lime juice, chile, and ½ teaspoon salt in a medium bowl. Taste and adjust the seasoning. To make the crema, combine the mayonnaise, yogurt, lime zest and juice, and ½ teaspoon salt. Taste and adjust the seasoning. Set both aside.

When the salmon has finished cooking, let the steam release naturally for 5 minutes before turning the valve to Venting to quick-release any residual steam.

Carefully remove the lid and, using the steam rack handles, lift out the steam rack. Use tongs to transfer the salmon to a plate. When cool enough to handle, flake it into pieces with a fork.

To serve, divide the salmon evenly among 8 tortillas, top with the slaw, drizzle with crema, and sprinkle with cilantro. Serve right away with lime wedges alongside.

¾ teaspoon ancho chile powder

¼ teaspoon ground cumin

¼ teaspoon ground coriander

Kosher salt and freshly ground black pepper

1 lb (500 g) salmon, skin on

1 cup (240 ml) water

FOR THE SLAW

½ lb (250 g) brussels sprouts, shaved

½ cup (50 g) shredded red cabbage

¼ cup (25 g) sliced red onion

¼ cup (7 g) fresh cilantro leaves, chopped

2 tablespoons fresh lime juice

1 serrano chile, minced

FOR THE CREMA

½ cup (120 ml) mayonnaise

½ cup (125 g) Greek yogurt

2 teaspoons grated lime zest

1½ teaspoons fresh lime juice

FOR SERVING

Corn tortillas, fresh cilantro leaves, lime wedges

Shave brussels sprouts using a cheese shredder—an unexpected yet easy tool for cutting the small sprouts into thin shreds.

Steamed Halibut & Veggies in Parchment

Steaming fish inside a parchment packet does double duty, infusing the fillets with flavor and making cleanup easy. You can swap the halibut for any other white, meaty fish such as striped bass, haddock, or cod.

SERVES 4

2 tablespoons olive oil

1 teaspoon freshly grated lemon zest

2 tablespoons fresh lemon juice (about 1 lemon)

1 tablespoon minced shallot

1 teaspoon minced fresh thyme leaves

Kosher salt and freshly ground black pepper

4 halibut fillets (about 6 oz/180 g each)

1 bulb fennel, halved and thinly sliced, fronds reserved for serving

1 red bell pepper, seeded and thinly sliced

2 cups (475 ml) water

FOR SERVING
Steamed white or brown rice (page 112)

Fennel fronds

In a small bowl, mix the olive oil, lemon zest and juice, shallot, thyme, ½ teaspoon salt, and ¼ teaspoon pepper. Place the halibut fillets on one side of a large piece of parchment paper and drizzle the sauce evenly over the fish. Top each piece with sliced fennel and bell pepper and seal the parchment around the fish (see note below).

Pour the water into the Instant Pot® and place the fish in its parchment packet on the steam rack. Using the handles, lower the packet and steam rack into the pot. Lock the lid in place and turn the valve to Sealing. Press the Steam button and set the cook time for 3 minutes.

Let the steam release naturally for 5 minutes before turning the valve to Venting to quick-release any residual steam.

Carefully remove the lid and, using the steam rack handles, lift out the packet. Open the steam-filled parchment packet carefully and use tongs to transfer the fish, fennel, and peppers to a serving platter. Sprinkle with reserved fennel fronds and black pepper. Serve right away with rice alongside.

NOTE *To seal the fish in parchment paper, fold a large piece of parchment paper in half and cut it into a heart shape. Arrange the fish and vegetables on one side of the heart. Fold the uncovered half of the parchment over the fish. Starting at the top of the heart, begin to tightly fold the edges together. When you have reached the bottom of the heart, twist the paper to seal.*

Sesame Salmon & Soba Noodles

Marinated with honey and sesame and quickly cooked under pressure, salmon adds distinctive flavor, color, and nutrition to this Asian-inspired dish. To make it gluten-free, look for buckwheat soba noodles and swap in tamari for soy sauce.

SERVES 4

To make the marinade, in a small bowl or measuring cup, whisk together the vinegar, tamari, honey, sesame oil, garlic, and ginger. Place the salmon fillets in a shallow pan or baking dish and pour the marinade over the top. Cover with plastic wrap and marinate in the refrigerator for at least 30 minutes and up to 2 hours, turning occasionally to coat.

Transfer the salmon to the Instant Pot®, skin-side up, and pour the remaining marinade over the fish. Lock the lid in place and turn the valve to Sealing. Press the Pressure Cook button and set the cook time for 2 minutes at low pressure.

Meanwhile, bring a pot of water to a boil and cook the noodles according to the package directions. Drain well in a colander set in the sink, rinse with cold water, and drain again. Set aside.

When the fillets have finished cooking, let the steam release naturally for 5 minutes, then turn the valve to Venting to quick-release any residual steam. Remove the lid and use tongs to transfer the salmon to a serving platter. Press the Cancel button to reset the program.

Press the Sauté button and simmer the cooking liquid until it has thickened, 3–4 minutes. Transfer the sauce to a small bowl; set aside.

Add the oil, sliced bok choy, and a splash of water to the hot pot and cook until tender, about 3 minutes.

Transfer the noodles, vegetables, and salmon to a serving platter. To serve, spoon the sauce over the salmon, and top with sesame seeds and green onions.

FOR THE MARINADE
¼ cup (60 ml) rice vinegar

2 tablespoons tamari
or coconut aminos

1 tablespoon honey

2 tablespoons toasted
sesame oil

1 clove garlic, minced
or grated

2-inch (5-cm) piece of
ginger, peeled and grated
(about 1 tablespoon)

1 lb (500 g) salmon, skin on,
cut into 4 fillets

1 package (9½ oz/270 g)
soba noodles

1 tablespoon avocado or
canola oil

2 cups (150 g) sliced bok
choy or other firm, green
vegetable

FOR SERVING
Toasted sesame seeds

Chopped green onions

Substitute any firm, white fish fillet, such as halibut or sea bass, for the salmon, if you wish.

Fish Flavors

Most varieties of fish don't have much of a taste on their own,
but they take on spices and seasonings very well. Try these recipes with
any sturdy fish, such as halibut, snapper, Arctic char, salmon, or
sea bass, then add your favorite grains (page 114), steamed rice (page 112),
and/or veggies (page 106) to complete the meal.

SERVES 4

CHILE & LIME

In a small bowl, mix together the marinade ingredients.

Place the fish on a large piece of parchment paper, season with salt, and drizzle the marinade evenly over the fish. Seal the parchment around the fish (see Note, page 61).

Pour the water into the Instant Pot® and place the fish in its parchment packet on the steam rack. Using the handles, lower the packet and steam rack into the pot. Lock the lid in place and turn the valve to Sealing. Press the Steam button and set the cook time for 3 minutes. Let the steam release naturally for 5 minutes before turning the valve to Venting to quick-release any residual steam.

Carefully remove the lid and, using the steam rack handles, lift out the packet. Open the steam-filled parchment packet carefully and use tongs to transfer the fish to a serving platter.

FOR THE MARINADE

2 tablespoons olive oil

1 clove garlic, thinly sliced

1 serrano chile, seeded and finely chopped

1 teaspoon grated lime zest

1 tablespoon fresh lime juice

4 firm fish fillets, such as halibut, snapper, salmon, black cod, or Arctic char (about 6 oz/180 g each)

Kosher salt

2 cups (500 ml) water

SOY & GINGER

In a small bowl, mix together the marinade ingredients.

Place the fish fillets in a shallow pan or baking dish and pour the marinade over the top. Cover with plastic wrap and marinate in the refrigerator for at least 30 minutes and up to 2 hours, turning occasionally to coat.

Transfer the fish to the Instant Pot®, skin-side up, and pour the remaining marinade over the fish. Lock the lid in place and turn the valve to Sealing. Press the Pressure Cook button and set the cook time for 2 minutes at low pressure.

Let the steam release naturally for 5 minutes, then turn the valve to Venting to quick-release any residual steam. Carefully remove the lid and use tongs to transfer the fish to a serving platter. Spoon the sauce over the fish and serve.

FOR THE MARINADE

1 tablespoon peeled and grated fresh ginger

1 shallot, minced

2 tablespoons sugar

¼ cup (60 ml) soy sauce, tamari, or coconut aminos

¼ cup (60 ml) fresh lime juice

1 lb (500 g) salmon or firm white fish, skin on, cut into 4 fillets

LEMON & HERB

In a small bowl, mix together the marinade ingredients.

Place the fish on a large piece of parchment paper, season with salt and pepper, and drizzle the marinade evenly over the fish. Seal the parchment around the fish (see Note, page 61).

Pour the water into the Instant Pot® and place the fish in its parchment packet on the steam rack. Using the handles, lower the packet and steam rack into the pot. Lock the lid in place and turn the valve to Sealing. Press the Steam button and set the cook time for 3 minutes. Let the steam release naturally for 5 minutes before turning the valve to Venting to quick-release any residual steam.

Carefully remove the lid and, using the steam rack handles, lift out the packet. Open the steam-filled parchment packet carefully and use tongs to transfer the fish to a serving platter.

FOR THE MARINADE

2 tablespoons olive oil

2 tablespoons fresh lemon juice

1 teaspoon grated lemon zest

1 shallot, minced

1 tablespoon minced fresh marjoram or oregano

4 firm fish fillets, such as halibut, snapper, salmon, black cod, or Arctic char (about 6 oz/180 g each)

Kosher salt and freshly ground black pepper

2 cups (500 ml) water

Korean Steak & Brown Rice Bowl with Quick Pickled Veggies

A rich marinade of onion, soy, sesame, ginger, and pear tenderizes beef chuck and imbues it with a heady flavor. To thicken the sauce, mix 1 tablespoon each cornstarch and water and add it to the sauce before the final simmer.

SERVES 6

To make the marinade, in a blender or food processor, combine the onion, soy sauce, brown sugar, sesame oil, mirin, garlic, ginger, pepper, and honey. Peel, core, and quarter the pear, then add it to the blender. Blend at medium speed until smooth. Place the beef in a shallow pan or baking dish and pour the marinade over the top. Cover tightly with plastic wrap and marinate in the refrigerator for at least 4 hours or up to 24 hours, turning occasionally to coat.

Place the meat in the Instant Pot® and pour the marinade over the top. Lock the lid in place and turn the valve to Sealing. Press the Pressure Cook button and set the cook time for 35 minutes at high pressure.

Meanwhile, make the pickled veggies: Put the onions and radishes in a medium bowl, add a pinch of salt, and cover with white wine vinegar. Let stand at room temperature for at least 15 minutes. (Store in an airtight container in the refrigerator for up to 2 weeks.)

Let the steam release naturally, or for at least 15 minutes, before turning the valve to Venting to quick-release any residual steam.

Carefully remove the lid and use tongs to transfer the meat to a plate. Let the meat cool slightly and then shred it into big chunks using two forks. Press the Cancel button to reset the program.

Press the Sauté button on the Instant Pot® and bring the sauce to a simmer. Cook until it starts to thicken, 8–10 minutes.

Divide the meat over bowls of steamed rice and spoon the sauce on top. Garnish each bowl with pickled vegetables and green onions.

FOR THE MARINADE
1 yellow onion, chopped

½ cup (120 ml) soy sauce, tamari, or coconut aminos

½ cup (100 g) firmly packed brown sugar

¼ cup (60 ml) toasted sesame oil

2 tablespoons mirin

8 cloves garlic

1-inch (2.5-cm) piece fresh ginger, peeled and sliced

2 teaspoons freshly ground black pepper

1 tablespoon honey

1 Asian or Bosc pear

2 lb (1 kg) boneless beef chuck, cut into 4 pieces

FOR THE PICKLED VEGGIES
1 red onion, thinly sliced

6 radishes, thinly sliced

Kosher salt

White wine vinegar

Steamed rice (page 112)

Sliced green onions

Lemongrass & Garlic Pork Chops

Thick-cut pork chops benefit from a light, lemongrass-infused marinade. A handful of fresh spinach added to the warm pot just before serving adds bright flavor, or you can sub in bok choy, shredded kale, or another leafy green.

SERVES 4

Use the flat side of your knife to firmly push down on each stalk of lemongrass until it splits. Then thinly slice the stalks.

To make the marinade, in a small bowl or measuring cup, whisk together the tamari, fish sauce, brown sugar, garlic, shallots, pepper, and lemongrass. Place the pork chops in a shallow pan or baking dish and pour the marinade over the top. Cover with plastic wrap and marinate in the refrigerator for at least 30 minutes and up to 2 hours, turning occasionally to coat.

Select Sauté on the Instant Pot® and heat the oil. Working in batches, add the pork chops, reserving the marinade, and brown evenly on both sides, 2–3 minutes per side. Transfer to a plate. Add the stock and use a wooden spoon to scrape up any browned bits. Add the reserved marinade and stir to combine. Return the pork and its juices to the pot. Press the Cancel button to reset the program.

Lock the lid in place and turn the valve to Sealing. Press the Pressure Cook button and set the cook time for 10 minutes at high pressure.

Let the steam release naturally, or for at least 10 minutes, before turning the valve to Venting to quick-release any residual steam.

Carefully remove the lid and use tongs to transfer the pork chops to a serving platter. Drain all but two tablespoons of cooking liquid from the pot. Press the Cancel button to reset the program.

Press the Sauté button and add the spinach. Cook until the spinach has wilted, 3–5 minutes. Transfer to the platter with the pork chops. Serve with rice alongside.

FOR THE MARINADE
2 stalks lemongrass, tough outer leaves removed

3 tablespoons tamari, soy sauce, or coconut aminos

3 tablespoons fish sauce

¼ cup (50 g) firmly packed brown sugar

6 cloves garlic, minced or grated

2 large shallots, minced

½ teaspoon freshly ground black pepper

4 bone-in, thick-cut pork chops (about 3 lb/1.4 kg)

1 tablespoon canola oil

1 cup (240 ml) chicken or beef stock (pages 120–121 or store-bought)

5 oz (150 g) baby spinach

FOR SERVING
Steamed white or coconut rice (pages 112–113)

Bruise then slice the
lemongrass stalks before
adding them to the marinade
to release their full flavor.

Offer sambal oelek
(Indonesian red chile paste),
Sriracha, or other chile sauce
for adding at the table.

Drunken Noodles with Beef

Lean cuts of meat, such as the top sirloin here, become surprisingly succulent when cooked under pressure. Chiles contribute flavor and spice. Adjust the heat to suit your taste, stirring in chile sauce or paste just before serving, if desired.

SERVES 4-6

Select Sauté on the Instant Pot® and heat 1 tablespoon of oil. Add the broccolini and bell pepper and toss with the oil. Add the water and cook, stirring occasionally, just until bright in color and almost tender, about 3 minutes. Transfer the vegetables to a plate.

Season the beef all over with salt and pepper. Heat 1 tablespoon oil and add the beef. Brown the beef evenly on both sides, about 4 minutes per side, then transfer to a plate. Add an additional tablespoon of oil if the pot gets too dry. Add the garlic and chiles and cook until fragrant, about 1 minute. Press the Cancel button to reset the program.

Add the stock, lime leaves, red pepper flakes, five-spice powder, fish sauce, sugar, and basil and stir to combine. Slice the beef into thin strips and return it to the pot. Stir to submerge the beef slices in the liquid. Lock the lid in place and turn the valve to Sealing. Press the Pressure Cook button and set the cook time for 12 minutes at high pressure.

Meanwhile, cook the noodles according to the package directions. Drain the noodles, transfer to a large bowl, and set aside.

Let the steam release naturally for about 12 minutes, then turn the valve to Venting to quick-release any residual steam. Press the Cancel button to reset the program.

Select Sauté and simmer the sauce until slightly thickened, 5-7 minutes. (See note, page 67). Remove and discard the lime leaves. Return the vegetables to the pot and stir until warmed through, about 2 minutes.

Add the beef, vegetables, and sauce to the noodle bowl and toss to combine. Serve right away.

Canola or avocado oil

1 head broccolini, cut into 1-inch (2.5-cm) pieces, rough stems discarded

1 red bell pepper, seeded and thinly sliced

2 tablespoons water

1 lb (500 g) top sirloin, in one piece

Kosher salt and freshly ground black pepper

2 cloves garlic, minced

2 Thai chiles, seeded and thinly sliced

1 cup (240 ml) beef or chicken stock (pages 120-121 or store-bought)

4 Thai lime leaves

¼ teaspoon red pepper flakes

½ teaspoon Chinese five-spice powder

2 tablespoons fish sauce

½ teaspoon coconut sugar

2 fresh basil leaves, preferably Thai, plus more for serving

1 package (16 oz/500 g) wide dried rice noodles

Shredded Chicken Shawarma Wraps

A creamy tahini sauce balances the curry-infused marinade in this classic Middle Eastern dish. Serve the chicken in whole-wheat wraps with torn romaine, sliced tomatoes, and onion, or sideline the wraps and up the lettuce for a main dish salad.

SERVES 4

To make the marinade, in a measuring cup, combine the olive oil, curry powder, cumin, garlic, lemon juice, 1 teaspoon salt, and ⅛ teaspoon pepper and stir to combine. Place the chicken in a shallow pan or baking dish and pour the marinade over the top. Cover tightly with plastic wrap and marinate in the refrigerator for at least 30 minutes or up to overnight, turning occasionally to coat.

Select Sauté on the Instant Pot®. Working in batches, add the chicken and marinade and brown evenly on both sides, about 3 minutes per side. Transfer to a plate as browned. Press the Cancel button to reset the program.

Add the stock, lock the lid in place, and turn the valve to Sealing. Press the Pressure Cook button and set the cook time for 10 minutes at high pressure.

Meanwhile, make the tahini sauce. In a small bowl, combine the yogurt, tahini, garlic, cilantro, lemon juice, ½ teaspoon salt, and ½ teaspoon pepper. Taste and adjust the seasoning as desired.

When the chicken has finished cooking, let the steam release naturally for 10 minutes before turning the valve to Venting to quick-release any residual steam.

Carefully remove the lid and use tongs to transfer the chicken to a plate. When cool enough to handle, shred it with two forks.

To serve, spread a wrap with tahini sauce, add chicken, lettuce, tomato slices, and onion (if desired) and fold to close. Repeat with the remaining wraps and serve right away.

FOR THE MARINADE
2 tablespoons olive oil

2 teaspoons curry powder

1 teaspoon ground cumin

2 cloves garlic, grated

1 tablespoon fresh lemon juice

Kosher salt and freshly ground black pepper

2 lb (1 kg) boneless, skinless chicken thighs

½ cup (120 ml) chicken stock (page 120 or store-bought)

FOR THE TAHINI SAUCE
¾ cup (180 ml) Greek yogurt

2 tablespoons tahini

1 clove garlic, grated

1 tablespoon chopped fresh cilantro

1 tablespoon fresh lemon juice

FOR SERVING
Whole-wheat wraps, romaine lettuce leaves, sliced tomatoes, thinly-sliced red onions (optional)

Ginger Chicken & Rice

In this easy, ginger-loaded dish, chicken and rice cook together at the same time for the perfect weeknight meal. The quick Asian marinade could also be used on fish or pork. Use any leftovers for Asian Chicken Salad (page 54).

SERVES 4

To make the marinade, in a measuring cup, combine the oyster sauce, soy sauce, vinegar, sesame oil, sugar, and ginger and stir to combine. Place the chicken in a shallow pan or baking dish and pour the marinade over the top. Cover tightly with plastic wrap and marinate in the refrigerator for at least 30 minutes or up to overnight, turning occasionally to coat.

Select Sauté on the Instant Pot® and heat the oil. Working in batches, add the chicken and marinade and brown evenly on both sides, about 3 minutes per side. Transfer to a plate as browned. Add the garlic and ginger and cook until fragrant, 1 minute. Add 1 tablespoon of stock and scrape up any browned bits. Add the rice and 1 teaspoon salt and cook, stirring continuously, until slightly toasted, about 2 minutes. Return the chicken and its juices to the pot, add the remaining stock, and stir to combine. Press the Cancel button to reset the program.

Lock the lid in place and turn the valve to Sealing. Press the Pressure Cook button and set the cook time for 8 minutes at high pressure.

Let the steam release naturally for 10 minutes, then turn the valve to Venting to quick-release any residual steam. Carefully remove the lid.

Serve with green onions or cilantro, if desired.

FOR THE MARINADE

1 tablespoon oyster sauce

2 tablespoons soy sauce, tamari, or coconut aminos

2 tablespoons rice vinegar

2 teaspoons toasted sesame oil

2 teaspoons sugar

1 teaspoon peeled and grated fresh ginger

2 lb (1 kg) boneless, skinless chicken thighs

1 tablespoon canola or avocado oil

2 cloves garlic, minced

2 teaspoons peeled and grated fresh ginger

2 cups (475 ml) chicken stock (page 120 or store-bought)

1½ cups (300 g) long-grain white rice, rinsed well and drained

Kosher salt

FOR SERVING
Sliced green onions or fresh cilantro leaves (optional)

Chicken Tacos with Avocado Spread

Spice-rubbed chicken thighs become fork-tender meat that is ideal for tacos. Spread a spoonful of citrusy avocado over each tortilla, then tuck in some of the chicken with a sprinkling of queso fresco and fresh cilantro for easy weeknight bites.

SERVES 6

In a small bowl, mix the cumin, chili powder, and 1 teaspoon salt. Place the chicken in a shallow pan or on a plate and toss with the spice mixture to coat.

Select Sauté on the Instant Pot® and heat the oil. Working in batches, add the chicken thighs and brown evenly on both sides, about 5 minutes per side. Press the Cancel button to reset the program.

Add the stock, lock the lid in place, and turn the valve to Sealing. Press the Pressure Cook button and set the cook time for 10 minutes at high pressure.

Meanwhile, make the avocado spread. In a small bowl, mash the avocados with the lime juice and season with salt and pepper. Set aside.

When the chicken has finished cooking, let the steam release naturally for 10 minutes before turning the valve to Venting to quick-release any residual steam.

Carefully remove the lid and use tongs to transfer the chicken to a plate. When cool enough to handle, shred it with two forks.

To serve, spread a tortilla with avocado spread, add chicken, beans (if desired), queso fresco, and cilantro. Repeat with the remaining tortillas and serve right away.

1½ tablespoons ground cumin

2 teaspoons chili powder

Kosher salt and freshly ground black pepper

6 boneless, skinless chicken thighs

2 tablespoons canola or avocado oil

½ cup (120 ml) chicken stock (page 120 or store-bought)

FOR THE AVOCADO SPREAD

2 ripe avocados, halved, pitted, and scooped from peel

2 teaspoons fresh lime juice

FOR SERVING

Pinto beans (page 118), optional

Corn tortillas, crumbled queso fresco, fresh cilantro leaves

Slip any remaining taco meat into a salad or soup for a nourishing snack.

Chicken Marinades

Chicken is a blank canvas for a myriad of flavors, from fragrant five spice to robust tandoori. Try any of these marinades on boneless, skinless chicken thighs or breasts. Cook boneless thighs at high pressure for 10 minutes and breasts for 4 minutes. (If using bone-in chicken, increase the cooking time to 15 minutes for thighs and 7 minutes for breasts.) Then pair with your favorite rice (page 112), grains (page 114), beans (page 118), and/or veggies (page 106).

SERVES 4

FIVE SPICE

In a small bowl, mix together the marinade ingredients.

Season the chicken lightly with salt. Place in a shallow pan or baking dish and pour the marinade over the top. Cover with plastic wrap and marinate in the refrigerator for at least 30 minutes and up to 2 hours, turning occasionally to coat.

Add the chicken and marinade to the Instant Pot®. Lock the lid in place and turn the valve to Sealing. Press the Pressure Cook button and set the cook time for 10 minutes (for chicken thighs) or 4 minutes (for chicken breasts) at high pressure. Let the steam release naturally for 10 minutes before turning the valve to Venting to quick-release any residual steam. Carefully remove the lid and use tongs to transfer the chicken to a serving plate.

FOR THE MARINADE
½ cup (120 ml) freshly squeezed orange juice (from 1 large orange)

2 tablespoons soy sauce, tamari, or coconut aminos

2 tablespoons fish sauce

1 tablespoon Chinese five-spice powder

2 teaspoons sambal oelek (Indonesian red chile paste) or Sriracha

1 teaspoon sugar

2 lb (1 kg) boneless, skinless chicken thighs or breasts

Kosher salt

TERIYAKI

In a small bowl, mix together the marinade ingredients.

Season the chicken with salt and pepper. Place in a shallow pan or baking dish and pour the marinade over the top. Cover with plastic wrap and marinate in the refrigerator for at least 30 minutes and up to 2 hours, turning occasionally to coat.

Select Sauté on the Instant Pot® and heat the oil. Working in batches, if needed, add the chicken, reserving the marinade, and brown evenly on both sides, 2–3 minutes per side. Add the stock and use a wooden spoon to scrape up any browned bits. Add the reserved marinade and stir to combine. Press the Cancel button to reset the program.

Lock the lid in place and turn the valve to Sealing. Press the Pressure Cook button and set the cook time for 10 minutes (for chicken thighs) or 4 minutes (for chicken breasts) at high pressure. Let the steam release naturally for 10 minutes before turning the valve to Venting to quick-release any residual steam. Carefully remove the lid and use tongs to transfer the chicken to a serving plate.

FOR THE MARINADE
1 clove garlic, minced

1 tablespoon peeled and grated fresh ginger

½ cup (60 ml) soy sauce, tamari, or coconut aminos

1 teaspoon toasted sesame oil

1 tablespoon sugar

¼ cup (60 ml) mirin

2½ lb (1.2 kg) boneless, skinless chicken thighs or breasts

Kosher salt and freshly ground black pepper

1 tablespoon canola or avocado oil

½ cup (120 ml) chicken stock (page 120 or store-bought)

LEMON CHIPOTLE

In a small bowl, mix together the marinade ingredients.

Season the chicken generously with salt and pepper. Place in a shallow pan or baking dish and pour the marinade over the top. Cover with plastic wrap and marinate in the refrigerator for at least 30 minutes and up to 2 hours, turning occasionally to coat.

Add the chicken, marinade, and stock to the Instant Pot®. Lock the lid in place and turn the valve to Sealing. Press the Pressure Cook button and set the cook time for 10 minutes (for chicken thighs) or 4 minutes (for chicken breasts) at high pressure. Let the steam release naturally for 10 minutes before turning the valve to Venting to quick-release any residual steam. Carefully remove the lid and use tongs to transfer the chicken and sauce to a serving plate. Sprinkle with basil and serve.

FOR THE MARINADE

1 tablespoon Dijon mustard

1 tablespoon fresh lemon juice

3 tablespoons olive oil

½ shallot, minced

1 teaspoon minced canned chipotle chiles in adobo, with 1 teaspoon sauce

2 lb (1 kg) boneless, skinless chicken breasts or thighs

Kosher salt and freshly ground black pepper

½ cup (120 ml) chicken stock (page 120 or store-bought)

Chopped fresh basil, for serving

TANDOORI

In a small bowl, mix together the marinade ingredients.

Place the chicken in a shallow pan or baking dish and pour the marinade over the top. Cover with plastic wrap and marinate in the refrigerator for at least 1 hour and up to 24 hours, turning occasionally to coat.

Add the chicken, marinade, and stock to the Instant Pot®. Lock the lid in place and turn the valve to Sealing. Press the Pressure Cook button and set the cook time for 4 minutes at high pressure. Let the steam release naturally for 10 minutes before turning the valve to Venting to quick-release any residual steam. Carefully remove the lid and use tongs to transfer the chicken to a serving plate.

FOR THE MARINADE

¾ cup (180 ml) plain whole-milk yogurt

1 teaspoon ground cumin

1 teaspoon ground turmeric

½ teaspoon smoked paprika

½ teaspoon saffron threads

½ teaspoon ground cinnamon

½ teaspoon kosher salt

¼ teaspoon black pepper

1½ lb (700 g) boneless, skinless chicken breasts, cut into 1½-inch (4-cm) cubes

½ cup (120 ml) chicken stock (page 120 or store-bought)

Substitute the bone-in chicken thighs for boneless, if you wish, and reduce the cooking time to 10 minutes.

Chicken with Cider & Apples

Adding the apples to this comforting cold-weather dinner in two additions—with the chicken and just before serving—contributes flavor and chunky texture to the sweet-savory sauce. Serve over steamed rice or mashed potatoes.

SERVES 4–6

Pat the chicken dry with paper towels and season both sides generously with salt and pepper. Select Sauté on the Instant Pot® and heat the oil. Working in batches, cook the chicken, skin-side down, until nicely browned, about 5 minutes. Transfer to a plate. Add the shallots and cook until translucent and slightly soft, 3 minutes. Add the garlic and cook until fragrant, 1 minute. Add the cider, stock, and vinegar and stir to combine. Press the Cancel button to reset the program.

Return the chicken to the pot. Add half of the apples and the rosemary and stir to combine. Lock the lid in place and turn the valve to Sealing. Press the Pressure Cook button and set the cook time for 15 minutes at high pressure.

Let the steam release naturally, or for at least 10 minutes, before turning the valve to Venting to quick-release any residual steam.

Carefully remove the lid and use tongs to transfer the chicken to a plate. Press the Cancel button to reset the program. Press the Sauté button, add the butter and the remaining apples, and cook until the sauce is slightly reduced, about 3 minutes. (The sauce will continue to thicken as it cools.) Return the chicken to the pot and stir to coat.

Serve over rice or potatoes, with sauce drizzled on top.

2½ lb (1.2 kg) bone-in, skin-on chicken thighs (about 6), excess fat trimmed

Kosher salt and freshly ground black pepper

1 tablespoon olive oil

3 shallots, sliced

2 cloves garlic, minced

1 cup (240 ml) apple cider

½ cup (120 ml) chicken stock (page 120 or store-bought)

2 tablespoons apple cider vinegar

2 Granny Smith apples, peeled, cored, and cut into wedges

1 sprig fresh rosemary leaves

½ tablespoon unsalted butter

FOR SERVING
Steamed rice (page 112), steamed potatoes (page 108), or mashed potatoes

Turkey Meatballs with Tomato Sauce

Serve these low-fat, Italian-spiced meatballs with Spaghetti Squash (page 111) or cooked pasta. Skip the Parmesan to make it dairy-free.

SERVES 4–6

To make the meatballs, select Sauté on the Instant Pot® and heat the olive oil. Add the onion and cook, stirring occasionally, until softened, about 3 minutes. Add the garlic and cook, stirring occasionally, until fragrant, about 1 minute. Transfer to a small bowl and let cool. Press the Cancel button to reset the program while you shape the meatballs.

Line a rimmed baking sheet with parchment paper. In a large bowl, combine the egg, bread crumbs, cheese, basil, red pepper flakes, 2 teaspoons salt, 1 teaspoon black pepper, the meat, and the cooked onion mixture. Using your hands or a wooden spoon, stir gently to combine (be careful not to overmix, or the meat will become tough). Take a heaping tablespoon of meat and, using slightly wet hands, roll it between your palms to form a 1-inch (2.5-cm) ball. Place each ball on the prepared baking sheet and set aside.

To make the tomato sauce, in a large bowl, whisk together the stock, tomatoes, tomato paste, basil, oregano, red pepper flakes, olive oil, mustard, ½ teaspoon salt, and ½ teaspoon black pepper.

Pour the tomato sauce into the pot. Add the meatballs and turn to coat them in the sauce. Lock the lid in place and turn the valve to Sealing. Press the Pressure Cook button and set the cook time for 10 minutes at high pressure.

Let the steam release naturally for 10 minutes, then turn the valve to Venting to quick-release any residual steam. Carefully remove the lid and stir. Taste and adjust the seasoning as needed.

Serve the meatballs and sauce over spaghetti squash or pasta. Garnish with Parmesan, basil leaves, and freshly ground black pepper.

FOR THE MEATBALLS

1 tablespoon olive oil

1 small yellow onion, chopped

3 cloves garlic, minced

1 large egg, lightly beaten

¼ cup (25 g) dried bread crumbs

½ cup (60 g) grated Parmesan cheese, plus more for serving

1 tablespoon chopped fresh basil, plus leaves for serving

½ teaspoon red pepper flakes

Kosher salt and freshly ground black pepper

1 lb (450 g) ground turkey

FOR THE TOMATO SAUCE

½ cup (120 ml) chicken stock (page 120 or store-bought)

1 can (28 oz/800 g) crushed tomatoes

½ cup (120 g) tomato paste

1 tablespoon chopped fresh basil

2 teaspoons dried oregano

1 teaspoon red pepper flakes

¼ cup (60 ml) olive oil

1 tablespoon Dijon mustard

Kosher salt and freshly ground black pepper

Tofu Rice Bowl

This satisfying bowl features a great combo of textures—especially in its mix of crispy broccolini and silky tofu topped with crunchy nuts.

SERVES 4

To make the marinade, in a measuring cup or pitcher, whisk together the ginger, lime juice, tamari, chile sauce, and sesame oil. Reserve about 2 tablespoons of the marinade. Cut the tofu into 1-inch (2.5-cm) cubes. Place the tofu cubes in a large bowl, pour the remaining marinade over the top, and toss gently to combine. Set aside.

Select Sauté on the Instant Pot® and heat the oil. Add the broccolini, ¼ teaspoon salt, and a few grindings of pepper, and toss with the oil. Add the reserved 2 tablespoons marinade and 1 tablespoon water and cook, stirring occasionally, just until the veggies are bright green and tender, about 3 minutes. Use tongs or a large slotted spoon to transfer the veggies to the bowl with the tofu. Press the Cancel button to reset the program.

Add the rice, 1 cup (240 ml) water, and ½ teaspoon salt to the pot and stir to combine. Lock the lid in place and turn the valve to Sealing. Press the Pressure Cook button and set the cook time for 4 minutes at high pressure.

Let the steam release naturally for about 10 minutes, then turn the valve to Venting to quick-release any residual steam. Add the rice to the bowl with the tofu and veggies and use a large spoon to mix them all together gently.

To serve, spoon the tofu mixture into individual bowls and top with chopped nuts and herbs as desired.

FOR THE MARINADE

1 tablespoon peeled and grated fresh ginger

2 tablespoons fresh lime juice

2 tablespoons tamari, soy sauce, or coconut aminos

1 teaspoon chile sauce such as Sriracha or sambal oelek

2 teaspoons toasted sesame oil

1 package (14–16 ounces) firm or extra firm tofu, drained and patted dry

1 tablespoon canola or avocado oil

1 lb (450 g) broccolini, trimmed and cut into 2-inch (5-cm) pieces

Kosher salt and freshly ground black pepper

1 cup (240 ml) plus 1 tablespoon water

1 cup (200 g) long-grain white rice, rinsed well and drained

FOR SERVING

Chopped nuts such as dry roasted peanuts, roasted almonds, or pistachios

Chopped fresh cilantro, fresh mint, and/or fresh basil leaves

Thai Veggie Curry

This coconut-milk curry will become your weeknight go-to since it only takes a few minutes to prepare, and the winter squash becomes meltingly tender in under five minutes. Round out the meal with steamed rice (page 112).

SERVES 4–6

Select Sauté on the Instant Pot® and heat the oil. Add the onion and bell pepper along with 1 teaspoon salt and ¼ teaspoon pepper until the veggies begin to soften, about 3 minutes. Add the curry paste and squash and stir until combined. Press the Cancel button to reset the program.

Add the coconut milk and stock to the pot and stir to combine. Lock the lid in place and turn the valve to Sealing. Press the Pressure Cook button and set the cook time for 4 minutes at high pressure.

Turn the valve to Venting to quick-release the steam. Carefully remove the lid and stir the curry. Taste and adjust the seasoning, if needed.

Serve over rice and top with basil.

2 tablespoons canola or avocado oil

1 yellow onion, chopped

1 red bell pepper, seeded and sliced

Kosher salt and freshly ground black pepper

2½ tablespoons red or yellow curry paste

2 lb (1 kg) butternut squash or pumpkin, peeled, seeded, and cut into 1-inch (2.5-cm) cubes

1 can (13.5 oz/400 ml) full-fat coconut milk

1 cup (240 ml) vegetable stock (page 121 or store-bought)

FOR SERVING
Steamed white or brown rice (page 112)

Basil leaves, preferably Thai

Farrotto Two Ways

Farro contributes both nutrients and earthy flavor to this riff on classic Italian risotto. Switch up the mix-ins according to the season, layering in peas and asparagus for spring and Parmesan and spinach for autumn.

SERVES 4–6

Select Sauté on the Instant Pot® and heat the oil. Add the shallots and garlic and cook, stirring occasionally, until softened, about 3 minutes. Add the farro and cook, stirring occasionally, until it smells nutty and starts to pop, about 3 minutes. Add the wine and cook, stirring occasionally with a wooden spoon to scrape up any browned bits. Cook until the wine is absorbed, then stir in the stock, thyme, and 1 teaspoon salt. Press the Cancel button to reset the program.

Lock the lid in place and turn the valve to Sealing. Press the Pressure Cook button and set the cook time for 10 minutes at high pressure. Let the steam release naturally for about 10 minutes, then turn the valve to Venting to quick-release any residual steam and carefully remove the lid. Remove and discard the thyme sprigs.

For Parmesan & Spinach Farrotto, stir the Parmesan, spinach, and 1 tablespoon of the tarragon into the farrotto until the spinach is wilted, and season with salt and pepper. Transfer to a serving bowl. Sprinkle with Parmesan and the remaining 1 tablespoon tarragon and serve right away.

For Asparagus & Pea Farrotto, press the Cancel button to reset the program. Trim the cut ends from the asparagus and cut the spears into ½-inch (12-mm) pieces. Select Sauté and stir in the peas and asparagus. Cook until the vegetables begin to soften and are warmed through, about 3 minutes. Stir in the cheese and parsley and season with salt and pepper. Transfer to a serving platter. Sprinkle with parsley and lemon zest and serve right away.

2 tablespoons olive oil

2 shallots, minced

2 cloves garlic, minced

1½ cups (315 g) farro

½ cup (120 ml) dry white wine

3 cups (700 ml) vegetable or chicken stock (pages 120–121)

3 fresh thyme sprigs

Kosher salt and freshly ground black pepper

FOR PARMESAN & SPINACH

¼ cup (30 g) freshly grated Parmesan cheese, plus more for serving

5 oz (150 g) spinach or kale

2 tablespoons chopped fresh tarragon

FOR ASPARAGUS & PEA

½ lb (250 g) asparagus

1 cup (150 g) English peas

¼ cup (30 g) freshly grated Asiago cheese, plus more for serving

1 tablespoon chopped fresh flat-leaf parsley, plus more for serving

Fresh lemon zest, for serving

Sweet Potatoes with Tzatziki

Cooking sweet potatoes under pressure yields a moist, creamy texture that's hard to duplicate with oven baking. Topped with a light and refreshing tzatziki sauce, the plain potato becomes a simple meal on its own, or a side dish paired with Quinoa, Lentil & Radicchio Salad (page 51).

SERVES 2–4

2 sweet potatoes

2 cups (475 ml) water

FOR THE TZATZIKI

1 cup (250 g) Greek yogurt

1 English cucumber, seeded, finely grated, and drained

½ teaspoon lemon zest

2 teaspoons fresh lemon juice

1 tablespoon chopped dill

Kosher salt and freshly ground black pepper

Chopped fresh flat-leaf parsley, for serving

Pierce the sweet potatoes all over with a fork. Pour the water into the Instant Pot® and insert the steam rack. Place the potatoes on the steam rack. Lock the lid in place and turn the valve to Sealing. Press the Pressure Cook button and set the cook time for 20 minutes at high pressure.

Meanwhile, make the tzatziki. In a small bowl, combine the yogurt, cucumber, lemon zest, lemon juice, dill, and ½ teaspoon salt. Stir to combine. Taste and adjust the salt as needed.

When the potatoes have finished cooking, let the steam release naturally for 10 minutes, then turn the valve to Venting to quick-release any residual steam. Carefully remove the lid and, using the steam rack handles, lift out the potatoes. Let cool slightly.

To serve, slice each potato in half and spoon tzatziki on each half. Sprinkle with pepper and parsley and serve.

Veggie Tacos

Once you get the hang of pressure cooking, you may find your fridge filling up with some of the easy-to-prepare staples in this recipe. Select your own favorite rice, beans, and veggies to tuck into these simple tacos, or use any leftovers and add to them with your choice of ingredients.

SERVES 4

Prepare the rice, beans, and veggies (if desired) as directed, if you don't have any left over from other meals.

To make the Pico de Gallo, in a small bowl, combine the tomatoes, onion, chile, cilantro, ½ teaspoon salt, and 1 tablespoon lime juice. Stir to mix well, taste, and adjust the salt and lime juice as needed. (Use right away or store in an airtight container in the refrigerator for up to 3 days.)

To assemble the tacos, place a layer of rice on each tortilla, dividing it evenly, followed by layers of beans and vegetables (if using). Top with cabbage and pico de gallo and sprinkle with cheese. Add a dollop of sour cream to each taco and garnish with cilantro.

1 cup (160 g) steamed rice (page 112)

1 cup (180 g) cooked beans (page 118)

1 cup (125 g) steamed vegetables (optional; page 106)

FOR PICO DE GALLO
2 plum tomatoes, seeded and diced

¼ white onion, diced

1 serrano or jalapeño chile, minced

2 tablespoons finely chopped fresh cilantro

Kosher or fine sea salt

Fresh lime juice

4 corn or flour tortillas, warm

1 cup (90 g) shredded red or green cabbage

4 oz (120 g) cotija, crumbled, or Mexican blend shredded cheese

Sour cream and cilantro, for serving

Olive Oil–Almond Cake (page 103)

DESSERTS

Apple Cranberry Yogurt Cake

Yogurt adds a wonderfully light texture to this pretty cake. Select a good baking apple to arrange on top or substitute the apples with firm-fleshed pears, such as Bosc or Anjou. If cranberries are unavailable, use blueberries instead.

SERVES 6–8

Lightly grease a 7-inch (18-cm) springform pan or 6-cup (1.5-L) Bundt pan with butter.

In a small bowl, whisk together the flour, baking powder, and salt. In a large bowl, whisk the eggs and sugar until combined. Whisk in the yogurt and vanilla, then whisk in the 4 tablespoons melted butter. Fold the flour mixture into the egg mixture with a rubber spatula, then fold in the cranberries. Pour into the prepared pan and place the apples in a single layer on the top of the batter. Cover with aluminum foil.

Pour the water into the Instant Pot® and place the pan on the steam rack. Using the handles, lower the pan and steam rack into the pot. Lock the lid in place and turn the valve to Sealing. Press the Pressure Cook button and set the cook time for 40 minutes at high pressure.

Let the steam release naturally for 10 minutes, then turn the valve to Venting to quick-release any residual steam. Carefully remove the lid and, using the steam rack handles, lift out the springform pan. Let the cake cool slightly before removing it from the pan.

Cut into wedges and serve.

4 tablespoons butter, melted, plus more for greasing

1½ cups (185 g) all-purpose flour

2½ teaspoons baking powder

¼ teaspoon kosher salt

2 large eggs, at room temperature

1 cup (200 g) sugar

1 cup (250 g) Greek or plain whole-milk yogurt

1 teaspoon vanilla extract

1 cup (100 g) fresh or thawed frozen cranberries, roughly chopped

1 Braeburn, Jonagold, Honeycrisp, Crispin, or Pink Lady apple, cored and cut into thin slices

1½ cups (350 ml) water

For an embellishment at serving time, stir vanilla extract, honey, and grated lemon zest into a small bowl of Greek yogurt for adding at the table, if you like.

Coconut Mango Sticky Rice

Making sticky rice is an easy task when using the pot-in-pot method. Mango is a traditional topping, but you can swap it for any sweet and juicy fruit. Alternatively, serve the rice with a savory dish, such as a Thai curry (page 84).

SERVES 4

Combine the rice and the 1 cup (240 ml) water in a stainless steel or glass bowl that will fit inside the Instant Pot®. Stir to make sure all of the rice is submerged in the water. Set the bowl on the steam rack. Pour the 2 cups (500 ml) water into the pot and, using the handles, lower the bowl and steam rack into the pot. Lock the lid in place and turn the valve to Sealing. Press the Rice button.

Let the steam release naturally for 12 minutes, then turn the valve to Venting to quick-release any residual steam. Carefully remove the lid and, using the steam rack handles, lift out the bowl. Drain the water from the inner pot. Press the cancel button to reset the program.

To make the coconut sauce, press the Sauté button. Add the coconut milk, maple syrup, and a generous pinch of salt to the pot. Whisk to break up any lumps. Cook until the milk starts to simmer, 2–3 minutes. (This step can also be done in a small saucepan on the stovetop while the rice is cooking.) Be careful not to boil the milk. Pour the milk into a measuring cup or pitcher and let cool slightly.

Divide the rice among four small coffee mugs, using a spoon to press it firmly into the mugs—it will be sticky! Pour ¼ cup (60 ml) warm sauce over the rice in each mug and let rest for a few minutes until the sauce is almost completely absorbed.

To serve, turn out each rice pudding onto a dessert plate (it's OK if some sauce runs out onto the plate), top with mango cubes, and sprinkle with coconut flakes.

1 cup (200 g) short-grain white rice, rinsed and drained

1 cup (240 ml) water, plus 2 cups (500 ml) for steaming

FOR THE COCONUT SAUCE
1 cup (240 ml) full-fat coconut milk

1 tablespoon maple syrup

Kosher salt

1 ripe mango, cut into 1-inch (2.5-cm) cubes

Toasted coconut flakes, for serving

Steamed Stone Fruit Puddings

Classic British steamed puddings are so much quicker and easier to manage in the Instant Pot® than in a traditional steam-water bath. Use any summer stone fruits in this cakelike dessert, or substitute apples and pears in autumn.

SERVES 4

Grease four 4- to 6-oz (120- to 180-ml) ramekins with butter.

In the bowl of a food processor, combine the flour, brown sugar, the 4 tablespoons butter, the ginger, cardamom, baking soda, and salt. Pulse until the butter forms crumbles. Add the egg and milk and pulse until smooth. The batter will be thick and slightly sticky.

Use a rubber spatula to scrape the batter from the food processor. Spoon it into the prepared ramekins, dividing it evenly. Arrange the fruit slices on top of the batter, dividing them evenly. Sprinkle each ramekin with 1 teaspoon turbinado or granulated sugar. Cover each ramekin with aluminum foil.

Pour the water into the Instant Pot® and place the ramekins on the steam rack. If they don't all fit in one layer, cook them in batches or make a second layer with the remaining ramekin(s), staggering them to balance on top of the first layer. Using the handles, lower the ramekins and steam rack into the pot. Lock the lid in place and turn the valve to Sealing. Press the Pressure Cook button and set the cook time for 24 minutes at high pressure.

Turn the valve to Venting to quick-release the steam. Carefully remove the lid and, using the steam rack handles, lift out the ramekins. Let the puddings cool slightly.

Serve the puddings warm, either still in the ramekins or after using an offset spatula to gently loosen the edges and turn them out onto dessert plates.

4 tablespoons (60 g) unsalted butter, cut into cubes, plus more for greasing the ramekins

1 cup (115 g) all-purpose flour

⅓ cup (75 g) firmly packed brown sugar

1 teaspoon ground ginger

1 teaspoon ground cardamom

1 teaspoon baking soda

¼ teaspoon salt

1 large egg, at room temperature, lightly beaten

⅓ cup (75 ml) milk

½ lb (250 g) stone fruit, such as peaches, plums, or nectarines, pitted and cut into thin slices

4 teaspoons turbinado or granulated sugar

2 cups (500 ml) water

Zucchini Bread

Cooking with steam heat and adding coconut oil to the batter results in an evenly moist cake with just the right amount of sweetness. Source a 6-cup (1.5-L) Bundt pan online, or try a 7-inch (18-cm) springform pan in a pinch.

SERVES 6–8

Grease a 6-cup (1.5-L) Bundt pan with nonstick cooking spray.

In a small bowl, whisk together the flour, baking powder, baking soda, cinnamon, nutmeg, and salt. In a medium bowl, whisk together the eggs, coconut oil, brown sugar, and vanilla. Fold in the zucchini using a rubber spatula. Gently fold the flour mixture into the egg mixture, being careful not to overmix the batter. Pour into the prepared pan and cover with aluminum foil.

Pour the water into the Instant Pot® and place the Bundt pan on the steam rack. Using the handles, lower the pan and steam rack into the pot. Lock the lid in place and turn the valve to Sealing. Press the Pressure Cook button and set the cook time for 35 minutes at high pressure.

Let the steam release naturally for 10 minutes, then turn the valve to Venting to quick-release any residual steam. Carefully remove the lid and, using the steam rack handles, lift out the Bundt pan. Let the bread cool slightly before using an offset spatula to gently loosen the edges and remove it from the pan.

Cut into slices and serve.

Nonstick cooking spray

1½ cups (175 g) all-purpose flour

2 teaspoons baking powder

1 teaspoon baking soda

1½ teaspoons cinnamon

½ teaspoon nutmeg

½ teaspoon salt

2 eggs

½ cup (120 ml) coconut oil, melted and cooled

1 cup (215 g) firmly packed brown sugar

1 teaspoon vanilla extract

2 medium zucchini, grated, excess water drained on a paper towel (about 2 cups/225 g grated)

2 cups (500 ml) water

Mini Ricotta Cheesecakes with Fresh Berries

A blend of ricotta cheese and Greek yogurt offers a lighter option than cream cheese in these single-serving cheesecakes. Garnish them with fresh fruit, or make a quick sauce of sweetened fresh berries warmed over medium heat.

SERVES 6

To make the crust, lightly grease the sides of six 3-inch (7.5-cm) cake pans with removable bottoms or a 7-inch (18-cm) springform pan with butter. In a medium bowl, mix the ground almonds, sugar, lemon zest, and the 4 tablespoons butter until combined. Divide evenly among the prepared pan(s), press the crust into the pan(s), and set aside.

In a food processor, mix the ricotta, yogurt, the ⅓ cup (70 g) sugar, and vanilla until blended. Add the eggs, one at a time, and beat just until incorporated. (Do not overmix.) Pour over the crust in the pan(s) and cover each with aluminum foil.

Pour the water into the Instant Pot® and place 3 of the small pans or the single large pan on the steam rack. Using the handles, lower the pan(s) and steam rack into the pot. Lock the lid in place and turn the valve to Sealing. Press the Pressure Cook button and set the cook time for 20 minutes at high pressure (for 3-inch/7.5-cm pans) or 35 minutes (for a 7-inch/18-cm pan).

Let the steam release naturally. Carefully remove the lid and, using the steam rack handles, lift out the pans. Transfer to a cooling rack, remove the foil, and let cool completely. Repeat with the remaining 3 pans, if using small pans. Cover each with plastic wrap and refrigerate for at least 2 hours or up to overnight.

To serve, remove the pan bottoms (or sides of the springform) and carefully remove the cheesecakes from the pans. Top with fresh berries and serve.

FOR THE CRUST
4 tablespoons unsalted butter, plus more for greasing

1 cup (100 g) ground almonds

¼ cup (50 g) sugar

2 teaspoons lemon zest

1 lb (500 g) whole-milk ricotta cheese

⅓ cup (75 g) Greek yogurt

⅓ cup (70 g) sugar

3 teaspoons vanilla extract

2 eggs, at room temperature

2 cups (500 ml) water

FOR SERVING
Fresh raspberries, blueberries, or blackberries, or a mix

For a saucelike finish,
crush some of the berries
with a pinch of sugar before
spooning them on top.

Coconut Milk Custard

Top these individually-sized custards with diced pineapple or mango to enhance their tropical appeal. Coconut milk contributes unique flavor, in addition to iron and zinc, but can be substituted with any of your favorite dairy milk or nut milk varieties.

SERVES 6

1 can (13.5 oz/400 ml) full-fat coconut milk

1 vanilla bean, split and scraped, or 2 teaspoons vanilla extract

5 large egg yolks

⅓ cup (70 g) sugar

Kosher salt

2 cups (500 ml) water

In a saucepan over medium heat, combine the coconut milk and the vanilla bean and its seeds and bring to a simmer. Turn off the heat, cover, and let steep for 15 minutes. Remove the vanilla bean. (If using vanilla extract, add it now and stir to combine.)

Meanwhile, in a large bowl, whisk together the egg yolks, sugar, and a pinch of salt. Quickly whisk about ¼ cup (60 ml) of the warm coconut-milk mixture into the egg yolk mixture, then whisk in the remaining milk mixture. Pour the mixture through a fine-mesh sieve placed over a large measuring cup or pitcher. Divide evenly among six 4-oz (120-ml) ramekins. Cover each ramekin with aluminum foil.

Pour the water into the Instant Pot® and place 3 of the ramekins on the steam rack. Using the handles, lower the ramekins and steam rack into the pot. Lock the lid in place and turn the valve to Sealing. Press the Pressure Cook button and set the cook time for 10 minutes at high pressure.

Let the steam release naturally for 10 minutes, then turn the valve to Venting to quick-release any residual steam. Carefully remove the lid and, using the steam rack handles, lift out the ramekins from the pot. Remove the foil and let cool slightly, then use a paper towel to carefully blot the layer of coconut oil that has risen to the top.

Repeat to cook the remaining 3 ramekins.

When all the custards are cooked, let cool to room temperature, cover with plastic wrap, and refrigerate until set, for at least 2 hours or up to 3 days. Serve chilled.

Fudge Brownie Cake

In this lightened-up version of dense chocolate cake, traditional butter and sugar are replaced by coconut oil and coconut sugar with no detraction to the wonderfully rich and fudgy texture. Cut into wedges and eat them with your hands like a brownie, or serve plated with a scoop of frozen yogurt alongside.

SERVES 8

Grease a 7-inch (18-cm) springform pan with nonstick cooking spray.

In a small bowl, whisk together the flour, cocoa powder, baking powder, and salt.

In a medium bowl, whisk together the eggs, sugar, melted coconut oil, vanilla, and espresso. Gently whisk the dry mixture into the wet mixture. Fold in the chocolate chips. Pour the mixture into the prepared pan and cover with aluminum foil.

Pour the water into the Instant Pot® and place the springform pan on the steam rack. Using the handles, lower the pan into the pot. Lock the lid in place and turn the valve to Sealing. Press the Pressure Cook button and set the cook time for 35 minutes at high pressure.

Let the steam release naturally for 15 minutes, then turn the valve to Venting to quick-release any residual steam. Carefully remove the lid and, using the steam rack handles, lift out the pan. Transfer to a cooling rack, remove the foil, and let cool completely.

To serve, remove the pan sides and cut the cake into wedges.

Nonstick cooking spray

1 cup (115 g) all-purpose flour

¼ cup (20 g) unsweetened cocoa powder

1 teaspoon baking powder

¼ teaspoon kosher salt

2 large eggs, at room temperature

1 cup (190 g) coconut sugar

5 tablespoons (75 ml) coconut oil, melted

½ teaspoon vanilla

1 espresso (or 2 tablespoons boiling water mixed with 1 tablespoon espresso powder), cooled

8 oz (225 g) regular or mini semisweet chocolate chips

2 cups (475 ml) water

Olive Oil–Almond Cake

Healthy olive oil, consisting primarily of monounsaturated fatty acids, is a welcome addition to cakes as it contributes both a tender crumb and a moist texture. Wheels of citrus make a juicy, colorful, and bright topping.

SERVES 6–8

Lightly grease a 7-inch (18-cm) springform pan with butter.

In a bowl, whisk the flours, baking powder, baking soda, salt, and ¼ cup (50 g) of the sugar. In a large bowl, using an electric mixer, beat the eggs until frothy. Add the remaining sugar and beat on high until thick and pale yellow, about 5 minutes. With the mixer on low, beat in the olive oil, orange zest, and vanilla. Fold the flour mixture into the egg mixture with a rubber spatula. Pour into the prepared pan and cover with aluminum foil.

Pour the water into the Instant Pot® and place the springform pan on the steam rack. Using the handles, lower the pan and steam rack into the pot. Lock the lid in place and turn the valve to Sealing. Press the Pressure Cook button and set the cook time for 35 minutes at high pressure.

Let the steam release naturally for 10 minutes, then turn the valve to Venting to quick-release any residual steam. Carefully remove the lid and, using the steam rack handles, lift out the springform pan. Let the cake cool slightly before removing it from the pan.

To serve, layer the orange slices in a circular pattern on top of the cake and drizzle with honey.

Unsalted butter, for greasing

1 cup (115 g) all-purpose flour

½ cup (50 g) almond flour

2 teaspoons baking powder

½ teaspoon baking soda

½ teaspoon kosher salt

1 cup (200 g) sugar

3 large eggs, at room temperature

⅓ cup (75 ml) olive oil

1 tablespoon freshly grated orange zest

2 teaspoons vanilla extract

2 cups (500 ml) water

FOR SERVING

2 navel or blood oranges, peeled with a knife and thinly sliced

Honey, for drizzling

Polenta (page 116)

HEALTHY BASICS

Quick Steamed Veggies

Instant Pot® steaming is a great choice for cooking vegetables, particularly hearty root vegetables, which are ready in half the amount of time required for other cooking methods. A quick, creamy dressing makes the ideal accompaniment.

SERVES 4–6

Pour the water into the Instant Pot®. Place the vegetables in a steamer basket or ovenproof bowl and set it on the steam rack. Using the handles, lower the steamer basket and steam rack into the pot. Lock the lid in place and turn the valve to Sealing. Press the Pressure Cook button and set the cook time for 4–6 minutes (about 2 minutes per pound/500 g) at high pressure.

Meanwhile, make the dressing. Combine the avocado, yogurt, oil, water, herbs, and lemon juice in a food processor or blender and process until smooth. Add salt and pepper to taste. Transfer to a small pitcher or jar.

When the vegetables have finished cooking, turn the valve to Venting to quick-release the steam. When the steam stops, carefully remove the lid and, using the steam rack handles, lift out the steamer basket.

To serve, transfer the vegetables to a large bowl and serve with dressing alongside.

1 cup (240 ml) water

2–3 lb (1–1.4 kg) vegetables, such as broccoli florets, cauliflower florets, broccolini, carrots, parsnips, squash, sugar snap peas, haricots verts, and/or asparagus, cut into similar-size pieces

FOR THE DRESSING
1 avocado, halved, pitted, and scooped from skin

¼ cup (65 g) plain or Greek yogurt

2 tablespoons avocado oil

⅓ cup (75 ml) water

½ cup (10 g) loosely packed fresh dill, parsley, or cilantro sprigs, or a combo

¼ cup (60 ml) fresh lemon juice

Kosher salt and freshly ground black pepper

Quick Steamed Potatoes

This foolproof method will work with any variety of potato—just be sure to cut the potatoes into 2-inch (5-cm) pieces. Try red new potatoes in potato salad (see recipe below) for a low-fat addition to a barbecue, picnic, or workday lunch.

SERVES 6

Pour the water into the Instant Pot® and insert the steam rack. Put the potatoes in a steamer basket and set it on the rack. Lock the lid in place and turn the valve to Sealing. Press the Pressure Cook button and set the time for 8 minutes at high pressure.

Turn the valve to Venting to quick-release the steam. When the steam stops, carefully remove the lid. Transfer the potatoes to a serving bowl. Toss with a few pats of butter, if using, season with salt and pepper, and serve, or use as desired.

2 cups (475 ml) water

3 lb (1.5 kg) potatoes, such as russet or Yukon gold, cut into 2-inch (5-cm) cubes

Unsalted butter, for serving (optional)

Kosher salt and freshly ground black pepper

VARIATION

Quick Potato Salad: *In a medium bowl, stir together ⅓ cup (35 g) thinly sliced red onion and 3 tablespoons red wine vinegar. Let stand until the onion softens slightly, about 5 minutes. In a small bowl, whisk together 1 tablespoon red wine vinegar, ¼ cup (60 ml) olive oil, and 2 tablespoons Dijon mustard. Stir into the onion mixture and season with salt and pepper. Set the vinaigrette aside.*

In a large bowl, combine 3 lb (1.5 kg) quick-steamed Yukon gold, fingerling, or new potatoes (see above), 6 thinly sliced radishes, and the vinaigrette and toss to combine. Season with salt and pepper. Top the potato salad with 2 peeled and sliced large hard-boiled eggs (see right) and 2 tablespoons coarsely chopped fresh dill. Serve warm or at room temperature, or refrigerate up to overnight and serve chilled.

Hard & Soft-Boiled Eggs

Although cooking eggs in a pressure cooker takes about the same amount of time as it does to cook them on the stove, with this method they will be much easier to peel—and you don't have to watch a pot of boiling water. Adjust the cooking time for how soft or hard you'd like the yolk: 5 to 6 minutes will yield a bright, slightly runny yolk, while 7 to 8 minutes will produce a firm center.

SERVES 1–12

2 cups (475 ml) water

Up to 12 large eggs

Pour the water into the Instant Pot® and insert the steam rack. Carefully arrange the eggs on the rack, stacking them on top of one another if necessary. Lock the lid in place and turn the valve to Sealing. Press the Pressure Cook button and set the cook time for 5–6 minutes at low pressure for soft-boiled eggs and 7–8 minutes at low pressure for hard boiled.

While the eggs are cooking, prepare an ice bath. When the eggs are ready, let the steam release naturally for 5 minutes, then turn the valve to Venting to quick-release any residual steam. Carefully remove the lid and transfer the eggs to the ice bath. When the eggs are cool enough to handle, lift them from the water. Crack the egg shells and peel the eggs. Use as desired.

Spaghetti Squash

All you need is a fork to make thin and tender strands of spaghetti squash, which is a healthful stand-in for pasta. Top a big bowl of it with any of your favorite sauces, such as marinara, pesto, or Bolognese.

SERVES 4–6

Pour the water into the Instant Pot®. Place the squash halves, cut-side down, in a steamer basket and set it on the steam rack. Using the handles, lower the steamer basket and steam rack into the pot. Lock the lid in place and turn the valve to Sealing. Press the Pressure Cook button and set the cook time for 4–6 minutes at high pressure (about 2 minutes per pound/500 g).

Let the steam release naturally for 5 minutes, then turn the valve to Venting to quick-release any residual steam. Carefully remove the lid and, using the steam rack handles, lift out the steamer basket. Transfer the squash to a cutting board. Gently run a fork along the inside of the squash to scrape the flesh free from the skin and transfer the strands to a bowl. Drizzle the squash with olive oil and season with salt and pepper. Serve warm with your favorite sauce.

TIP *Skip the olive oil and serve the spaghetti squash simply with butter and grated Parmesan cheese, seasoned with a little salt and a few grinds of pepper.*

3 cups (700 ml) water

1 medium spaghetti squash (2–3 lb/1–1.5 kg), halved crosswise and seeded

Olive oil

Kosher salt and freshly ground black pepper

Rice

Cooking rice can be a daunting task, not to mention a long one, when it comes to brown and wild rice varieties. This method is is quick and can be easily adjusted for your texture preference. If you like softer rice, add ¼ cup (60 ml) more water to the pot at the beginning, or let the steam release naturally for a longer period of time.

MAKES ABOUT 4 CUPS (640 G)

WHITE RICE

Combine the rice, water, and salt in the Instant Pot®. Lock the lid in place and turn the valve to Sealing. Press the Pressure Cook button and set the cook time for 4 minutes at high pressure.

Let the steam release naturally for 10 minutes, then turn the valve to Venting to quick-release any residual steam. Carefully remove the lid and fluff the rice with a fork. If the rice feels too moist, place a dish towel over the pot and let the steam evaporate for a few minutes longer, until your desired texture is reached.

2 cups (400 g) long-grain white rice, such as jasmine or basmati

2 cups (475 ml) water

½ teaspoon kosher salt

MAKES ABOUT 4 CUPS (808 G)

BROWN RICE

Combine the rice, water, and salt in the Instant Pot®. Lock the lid in place and turn the valve to Sealing. Press the Pressure Cook button and set the cook time for 15 minutes at high pressure.

Let the steam release naturally for 10 minutes, then turn the valve to Venting to quick-release any residual steam. Carefully remove the lid and fluff the rice with a fork. If the rice feels too moist, place a dish towel over the pot and let the steam evaporate for a few minutes longer, until your desired texture is reached.

2 cups (370 g) long-grain brown rice

2½ cups (600 ml) water

½ teaspoon kosher salt

WILD RICE

Combine the rice, water, and salt in the Instant Pot®. Lock the lid in place and turn the valve to Sealing. Press the Pressure Cook button and set the cook time for 30 minutes at high pressure.

Let the steam release naturally for 10 minutes, then turn the valve to Venting to quick-release any residual steam. Carefully remove the lid and fluff the rice with a fork. If the rice feels too moist, place a dish towel over the pot and let the steam evaporate for a few minutes longer, until your desired texture is reached.

V **GF** **VG** **DF** **LF**

1 cup (160 g) wild rice

2 cups (475 ml) water

1 teaspoon kosher salt

COCONUT RICE

Combine the rice, coconut milk, water, sugar, and salt in the Instant Pot®. Lock the lid in place and turn the valve to Sealing. Press the Pressure Cook button and set the cook time for 4 minutes at high pressure.

Let the steam release naturally for 10 minutes, then turn the valve to Venting to quick-release any residual steam. Carefully remove the lid and fluff the rice with a fork. If the rice feels too moist, place a dish towel over the pot and let the steam evaporate for a few minutes longer, until your desired texture is reached.

Serve with toppings, if desired.

2 cups (400 g) long-grain white rice, such as jasmine or basmati, rinsed well and drained

1 can (13.5 oz/400 ml) full-fat coconut milk

½ cup (120 ml) water

½ teaspoon sugar

½ teaspoon kosher salt

FOR SERVING
Toasted shredded coconut, chopped green onions, lime wedges

Hearty Grains

Grains are practically foolproof in the Instant Pot®, steaming quickly and evenly with no evaporation and requiring less liquid than if you cooked them on the stovetop. If you'd like a richer flavor, substitute chicken or vegetable stock for some or all of the water.

MAKES ABOUT 3 CUPS (330 G)

QUINOA

Put the quinoa, water, and salt in the Instant Pot®. Stir to combine.

Lock the lid in place and turn the valve to Sealing. Press the Pressure Cook button and set the cook time for 1 minute at high pressure.

Let the steam release naturally for 10 minutes, then turn the valve to Venting to quick-release any residual steam. Carefully remove the lid and fluff the quinoa with a fork.

1 cup (180 g) quinoa (red, white, or mixed), rinsed

1¼ cups (300 ml) water

½ teaspoon salt

FARRO

Put the farro, water, and salt in the Instant Pot®. Stir to combine.

Lock the lid in place and turn the valve to Sealing. Press the Pressure Cook button and set the cook time for 10 minutes at high pressure.

Let the steam release naturally for 10 minutes, then turn the valve to Venting to quick-release any residual steam. Carefully remove the lid.

1 cup (210 g) farro
1 cup (240 ml) water
½ teaspoon salt

PEARL BARLEY

Put the barley, water, and salt in the Instant Pot®. Stir to combine.

Lock the lid in place and turn the valve to Sealing. Press the Pressure Cook button and set the cook time for 20 minutes at high pressure for a chewier texture and up to 22 minutes for a soft texture.

Let the steam release naturally for 10 minutes, then turn the valve to Venting to quick-release any residual steam. Carefully remove the lid.

1 cup (200 g) pearl barley
2½ cups (600 ml) water
½ teaspoon salt

Polenta

Once the polenta has been stirred into the pot, you can set it and forget it—avoiding the nearly constant stirring required of traditional made on the stovetop polenta. Add butter and grated Parmesan cheese just before serving for a creamier texture and richer flavor, if you're feeling indulgent.

MAKES 2½ CUPS (625 G)

Select Sauté on the Instant Pot®. Add the liquid and 2 teaspoons salt and bring to a boil. Slowly stream in the polenta, whisking constantly to prevent clumping.

Press the Cancel button to reset the program. Lock the lid in place and turn the valve to Sealing. Press the Pressure Cook button and set the cook time for 8 minutes at high pressure.

Turn the valve to Venting to quick-release the steam. When the steam stops, carefully remove the lid.

Season the polenta to taste with salt and pepper. Stir in the butter and cheese, if desired, and serve.

4 cups (1 L) liquid, such as water, whole milk, and/or chicken stock (page 120 or store-bought)

Kosher salt and freshly ground black pepper

1 cup (160 g) polenta

2 tablespoons unsalted butter (optional)

½ cup (60 g) freshly grated Parmesan cheese (optional)

Beans, Chickpeas & Lentils

Although canned beans are very convenient, they just don't taste the same as the home-cooked kind. Last-minute cooks, rejoice! The absolute best part about preparing beans this way is that they don't need to be soaked ahead of time. For bigger batches, double the quantities of beans, water, and oil.

MAKES ABOUT 3 CUPS (540 G)

BASIC BEANS

Combine the beans, water, oil, and salt to taste in the Instant Pot®. Lock the lid in place and turn the valve to Sealing. Press the Beans/ Chili button and set the cook time for the cooking time designated in the chart below at high pressure.

Let the steam release naturally, or for at least 15 minutes, before turning the valve to Venting to quick-release any residual steam. When the steam stops, carefully remove the lid. Drain the beans in a colander set in the sink.

TIP *If you would prefer to soak your beans, soak 1 cup of beans in 4 cups (1 L) water for at least 4 hours or up to 12 hours, then cook them in their soaking water. They will cook in about half the time needed for unsoaked beans.*

1 cup (200 g) dried beans, chickpeas, or lentils, rinsed and picked over

4 cups (1 L) water

1 teaspoon canola oil

1–2 teaspoons kosher salt

COOKING TIMES FOR UNSOAKED BEANS & LENTILS

Green, Brown, or Black Lentils	15 minutes
Black Beans	20–25 minutes
Navy Beans	20–25 minutes
Pinto Beans	20–25 minutes
Cannellini Beans	35–40 minutes
Chickpeas	35–40 minutes

HUMMUS

Combine chickpeas, water, and 1 teaspoon salt in the Instant Pot®. Lock the lid in place and turn the valve to Sealing. Press the Beans/Chili button and set the cook time for 40 minutes at high pressure.

Let the steam release naturally, or for at least 15 minutes, before turning the valve to Venting to quick-release any residual steam. Carefully remove the lid and ladle 1 cup (240 ml) of the cooking liquid into a measuring cup. Drain the chickpeas in a colander set in the sink. Transfer the chickpeas to a blender or food processor. Add the garlic, lemon juice, tahini, cumin, 1 teaspoon of the smoked paprika, 1 teaspoon salt, and ½ cup (120 ml) of the reserved cooking liquid. Blend until almost smooth, adding more cooking liquid and scraping down the sides of the blender as needed. With the blender running, add the olive oil through the pour spout in a slow, steady stream until incorporated, about 2 minutes. Taste and add more salt if needed.

Transfer the hummus to a serving bowl, sprinkle with the remaining paprika and red pepper flakes, if using, drizzle with oil, and serve with pita and/or crudités.

1 cup (200 g) dried chickpeas

4 cups (1 L) water

Kosher salt

2 cloves garlic, chopped

Juice of 1 lemon

¼ cup (60 ml) tahini

¼ teaspoon ground cumin

2 teaspoons smoked paprika

¼ cup (60 ml) olive oil, plus more for serving

Red pepper flakes, for serving (optional)

FOR SERVING (OPTIONAL)
Pita bread or pita chips and/or crudités such as cauliflower florets, radishes, endive, daikon, bell peppers, carrots, cucumber, and cherry tomatoes

Homemade Stock

We can probably all agree that any dish made with homemade stock is better than those made with the store-bought version. While meat stocks used to require the better part of an afternoon to prepare, with the Instant Pot® you can shave hours off that time and eliminate the need to keep an eye on the stockpot. Store extra in the freezer to have on hand for quick weeknight meals.

MAKES ABOUT 3 QT (3 L)

CHICKEN STOCK

Season the chicken with the salt. Select Sauté on the Instant Pot® and heat the oil. Working in batches, brown the chicken on both sides, about 3 minutes per side. Transfer to a plate as browned. Add the onion and carrots to the pot and cook, stirring occasionally, until browned, about 2 minutes. Add 1 cup (250 ml) of the water and bring to a simmer, stirring occasionally with a wooden spoon to scrape up any browned bits. Press the Cancel button to reset the program.

Return the chicken to the pot and add the garlic, parsley, thyme, bay leaves, peppercorns, and the remaining 11 cups (2.75 L) water, ensuring that the pot is no more than two-thirds full. Lock the lid in place and turn the valve to Sealing. Press the Pressure Cook button and set the cook time for 60 minutes at high pressure.

Let the steam release naturally. Carefully remove the lid. Pour the stock through a fine-mesh sieve into a large bowl. Discard the solids. If desired, pour the broth into a fat separator to remove the fat (or chill the broth in the refrigerator until the fat solidifies on top, then remove it with a spoon). Let the stock cool completely, then ladle into airtight storage containers. Refrigerate for up to 4 days or freeze for up to 3 months.

3 lb (1.5 kg) chicken parts (drumsticks, backs, necks, and wings)

2 teaspoons kosher salt

1 tablespoon olive oil

1 yellow onion, quartered

2 carrots, cut into 3-inch (7.5-cm) pieces

12 cups (3 L) water

2 cloves garlic, smashed

3 fresh flat-leaf parsley sprigs

3 fresh thyme sprigs

2 bay leaves

¼ teaspoon whole black peppercorns

TIP *You can skip the browning step and put all of the raw ingredients into the pot instead, but keep in mind that the flavor will be milder.*

VEGETABLE STOCK

Combine all the ingredients in the Instant Pot®, ensuring when you add the water that the pot is no more than two-thirds full. Lock the lid in place and turn the valve to Sealing. Press the Pressure Cook button and set the cook time for 30 minutes at high pressure.

Let the steam release naturally. Carefully remove the lid. Pour the stock through a fine-mesh sieve into a large bowl. Discard the solids. Let the stock cool completely, then ladle into airtight storage containers. Refrigerate for up to 4 days or freeze for up to 3 months.

2 yellow onions, roughly chopped

2 ribs celery, roughly chopped

2 carrots, roughly chopped

1 cup (90 g) white button or cremini mushrooms, roughly sliced

4 cloves garlic, smashed

4 fresh flat-leaf parsley sprigs

2 bay leaves

1 teaspoon whole black peppercorns

10 cups (2.5 L) water

BEEF STOCK

Combine all the ingredients in the Instant Pot®, ensuring when you add the water that the pot is no more than two-thirds full. Lock the lid in place and turn the valve to Sealing. Press the Pressure Cook button and set the cook time for 2 hours at high pressure.

Let the steam release naturally. Carefully remove the lid. Pour the stock through a fine-mesh sieve into a large bowl. Discard the solids. If desired, pour the broth into a fat separator to removed the fat (or chill the broth in the refrigerator until the fat solidifies on top, then remove it with a spoon). Let the stock cool completely, then ladle into airtight storage containers. Refrigerate for up to 4 days or freeze for up to 3 months.

3 lb (1.5 kg) beef marrowbones, cracked by a butcher

2 thick slices (about 1 lb/ 450 g) meaty beef shin

2 carrots, roughly chopped

2 ribs celery, roughly chopped

1 large yellow onion, roughly chopped

4 fresh flat-leaf parsley sprigs

1 bay leaf

8–10 whole black peppercorns

8 cups (2 L) water

VARIATION

Bone Broth: *Roast the beef marrowbones for 30–40 minutes in a preheated 450°F (230°C) oven. Add 1–2 tablespoons apple cider vinegar to the pot with the other ingredients and cook at high pressure for 3 hours.*

Release the steam naturally. (The bone broth has cooked long enough if the bones crumble when touched and the tendons, cartilage, and connective tissue have dissolved.) Strain and store the broth as directed above.

Sesame Salmon &
Soba Noodles (page 62)

INDEX

Summer Garden
Soup (page 34)

HEALTHY INSTANT POT®

Conceived and produced by Weldon Owen International
in collaboration with Williams Sonoma, Inc.
3250 Van Ness Avenue, San Francisco, CA 94109

Printed in China
10 9 8 7 6 5 4 3 2

Library of Congress Cataloging-in-
Publication data is available.

ISBN: 978-1-68188-366-3

WELDON OWEN INTERNATIONAL
President & Publisher Roger Shaw
SVP, Sales & Marketing Amy Kaneko
Associate Publisher Amy Marr
Senior Editor Lisa Atwood
Art Director Marisa Kwek

Managing Editor Tarji Rodriguez
Production Manager Binh Au
Imaging Manager Don Hill

Photographer Erin Scott
Food Stylist Lillian Kang
Prop Stylist Claire Mack

Weldon Owen wishes to thank the following people for their
generous support in producing this book: Lisa Berman, Lesley
Bruynesteyn, Sarah Putman Clegg, Meghan Hildebrand, Josephine Hsu,
Veronica Laramie, Nicola Parisi, Elizabeth Parson, and Angela Williams.